Long forg
now remembered

A sequel to *Just an Essex Lad*

Ron Jeffries

First published in Great Britain in 2010
First printing June 2010

Some sections of the text were first published in the
BROADSHEET, the monthly newsletter of
St. Peter's Aldborough Hatch, Essex

A CIP catalogue record for this title is available from the British Library.
Paperback ISBN 978-0-9561877-1-0

Printed and bound in England by SPS Communications

Published at
37 Spearpoint Gardens,
Aldborough Road North,
Newbury Park,
ILFORD,
Essex IG2 7SX
United Kingdom
Email: ronjeffries@live.co.uk

To Graham, Heather and Richard
who may have spent their childhood years
wondering where their father was and
what he was getting up to.
Now they know.

By the same author

Programme Planning in the Scout Troop
The Outdoor Adventure Book for Cub Scouts and all boys
The Whizz Kids Book of Camping (with Paul Moynihan)
The Scout Troop – A handbook for Scout Leaders and Patrol Leaders
(with Paul Moynihan)
Just an Essex Lad – An autobiography

Contents

Introduction

*"The man who makes no mistakes does not usually make anything"**
Edward John Phelps (1822-1900)
Speech at the Mansion House, 24th January 1899

I published my autobiography – *Just an Essex Lad* – in March 2009, having retired eleven years earlier. The book sold out within nine months and is now out of print - and has, so I am assured by those who know about these things, acquired a premium value in the second-hand market. If you have a copy, hold onto it for its value will go up and up and up, and that's a fact. Although I could be persuaded to go for a reprint if there is the demand.

Having written some 230,000 words in *Just an Essex Lad* I thought I had covered everything, but it soon became obvious that I had not done so. Those who were reading my autobiography would telephone me – during the daytime, but occasionally at night, for the book proved a popular read with folk who had taken to their bed, having supped their Horlicks or Cocoa, and required something amusing to send them off to sleep in a good mood.

"You have forgotten to mention so-and-so," they would cry, *"and you have omitted the time you did this-that-and-the-other – or when this-that-or-the-other was done unto you."* And they were right.

And so *Long forgotten, now remembered* was born. Here I go back in time to rectify the errors of omission to tell of *The Great Gnome Saga* and *The Night I was driven to Gilwell Park for a sauna* and other similarly gripping and stirring – and, occasionally, harrowing - tales

I am grateful to a number of good friends who have reminded me of events and especially to those who have allowed me to use their recollections within these pages. My thanks to Christine Belcher, Stephen Brown, Roderic Findlay, Tony Kemp, Lionel King, Brian Lay, Colin Pryke, John Roper, John Sharrock, Bernard Thomas, Brian and Linda Watts - and those who names I have left out (to whom I offer my heartfelt apologies).

But what inspired me to publish this sequel? In late April 2010 I was in a Pound Shop in Ilford (one of many I would add) when a kindly gentleman, who was there with his wife, asked me when the sequel to *Just an Essex Lad* would be coming out? When I said I did not know he looked very sad indeed. He appeared so wistful and forlorn that I decided there and then not to disappoint him – or his wife. Will there be a follow-up to this sequel? I make no promises, but would merely state that writing is therapeutic when you are knocking on in years. It keeps me off the streets and from writing too many letters to the press.

The Great Gnome Saga

I was Editor of SCOUTING in the mid-1970s when the Postman came striding up the front garden path at Spearpoint Gardens with a well-wrapped cardboard box in his hand. Inside was a garden gnome, but it was no ordinary garden gnome for this was Nod-a-Lot, *The* Garden Gnome.

Standing some nine inches tall, Nod-a-Lot is a fine figure of a Garden Gnome. His coat is made of the very best material of a dusty azure blue hue, whilst his trousers are an attractive shade of saffron with a dash or two of red to mark them out from the crowd. In one hand Nod-a-Lot clutches a mushroom, whilst the other hand supports the substantial stalk of a Giant Sunflower, the latter being fully formed and glowing in dazzling yellow with lush green leaves. Nod's heavy boots are standing on a grassy knoll – as you might expect for he is very much the outdoor type of Garden Gnome.

How, you may well ask (and it is a fair question, to be sure), how do I know the detail of Nod-a-Lot's attire if the event in which he was involved took place long, long ago when Harold Wilson was Prime Minister and few of us had ever heard of the Falklands, whilst those who had could not find them on the map however hard they tried? Well, the fact is that Nod-a-Lot has spent the past thirty years or more standing on a tree stump at the bottom of my garden against the fence that separates our patch from that of Mr Dunmore, our neighbour – although he does find himself blown off from time to time (Nod-a-Lot, that is not Mr Dunmore) when the wind roars across the Green Belt of Fairlop Plan and whistles down the backs of the houses in Spearpoint Gardens, here in Aldborough Road North.

I trotted off down the garden to bring Nod-a-Lot indoors when writing this. Yvonne was somewhat alarmed, for she feared that a snail or two might have taken up residence in his body – for there is a snail-size aperture in the base of the grassy knoll. Sure enough there was a snail and it took Yvonne an inordinate amount of time to dislodge the fellow from his slumbers, but I waited patiently as Yvonne swilled him around in some warm water before flushing him out into the garden. Yvonne then insisted on giving Nod's inside a thorough cleaning with the best disinfectant money can buy in one of the many Pound Shops that have sprung up around here. At this very moment Nod sits on my desk (on a serviette, for he is leaking warm water from the snail-size aperture at the base of the grassy knoll and Yvonne would not thank me if the polished surface of my desk was spoiled), for I feel I need him near at hand as I recount this tale, one so highly charged with emotion, intrigue, mystery and the downright incredulous, that I fear I may burst into uncontrollable tearfulness as I write. Whilst I have stated the colours of his attire above, I should perhaps mention that his garb is not as pristine as it was all that time ago, but you can still work out which was once blue and which was saffron.

Inside the cardboard box – delivered by the postman all those years ago - Nod-a-Lot was stretched contentedly on a bed of tissue paper, grinning a gnome-like grin over his snow white beard that flowed to a point above his chest. A type-written note (for word processors and personal computers had yet to be invented, or if they had been, they were not available to the general populace) nestled below Nod-a-Lot's red pointed hat, which explained that Nod-a-Lot had recently retired and would be spending his twilight years in our garden, which had been specially selected as the profusion of lavender and rosemary bushes thereabouts would be very much to his liking.

Furthermore the note instructed Yvonne and me to be kind and generous to Nod-a-Lot, who had had a hard life and was looking forward to enjoying his remaining years on this earth amongst the dahlias and snap-dragons in the summer, and the daffodil and snowdrops in the spring.

He was, we were told, not a demanding Gnome, merely requesting that he might have the occasional wash-down with warm water, whilst a gentle spray up the aperture in the grassy knoll would also be appreciated, for he would not wish to become home to beetles, snails and slugs, although ladybirds would be most welcome, provided they wiped their feet on entering.

Nonplussed, but secretly rather proud of the fact that our front garden had been chosen from the many millions of English country gardens up and down the land as the final resting place of Nod-a-Lot, we placed him behind a lush green shrub where he would be sufficiently hidden not to be disturbed by inquisitive passers-by, but from where he would be able to observe the neighbours going about their daily lives and watch the twitching of the net curtains up, down and across the road.

A fine specimen

A day or so went by when the postman delivered a picture postcard with a full-colour view of an English seaside town. It was, indeed, a fine specimen of the genre and, before reading the message, I made a mental note to place it on the kitchen notice-board where we posted only the very best seaside picture postcards – unless the card happened to have been sent by Someone Important, in which case the quality of the card was immaterial and it went on the notice-board irrespective in a position of prominence where it might be seen by all who passed through our kitchen (as folk often do).

There was, indeed, nothing odd about our being the recipients of a picture postcard.

What should have sounded alarm bells ringing in our ears and up and down the length and breadth of Aldborough Road North here in Aldborough Hatch was the fact that the card was not addressed to Yvonne,

4

Nod-a-Lot, the Garden Gnome, has spent the past thirty years or more standing on a tree stump at the bottom of my garden next to the greenhouse and summerhouse (above). He is shy and prefers not to have his photograph taken, but will receive visitors by appointment.

nor to me, nor to our very young children, Graham, Heather and Richard – but to Nod-a-Lot, the Garden Gnome!

The handwritten message on the reverse purported to have been written by Nod-a-Lot's Elderly Aunt, who rejoiced under the name of Moan-a-Lot. In the message, the Good lady Gnome enquired after Nod-a-Lot's health and wished him every happiness in his well-deserved retirement. Yvonne and I smiled, pinned the card on the notice-board and thought no more about it – until a day or so later when a second postcard dropped onto the mat.

This, I seem to recall, although my memory is a little shaky as to the precise details, was posted in a Cathedral City somewhere in England and was signed by Kneel-a-Lot, the Vicar.

Not unnaturally, being a Vicar, Kneel-a-Lot included a prayer which he suggested Nod might use each night when he slipped his boots off, laid the sunflower down, rested his head on a bed of moss and covered his body with forest bark purchased from Shirley's farm-up-the-road. Again, Yvonne and I thought this a bit of fun, dismissing both postcards from our minds. But when another card arrived shortly afterwards, and another after that, and then yet another, we began to sit up and take notice.

Sinister

Each card was posted in a different town or city, but the messages on the back took on what might be considered to be more sinister tones for it was clear that whoever was writing these cards knew a thing or two about the movements and the goings-on within our family.

The writers would refer to an event that Yvonne or I had attended, or someone we had met. They knew what was happening at St. Peter's Church up the road from here and were aware of what our children and their friends were getting up to (well, some of the things anyway).

Many of Nod-a-Lot's cousins, nephews and nieces, aunts, uncles, friends and acquaintances started to send picture postcards to him – and these cards were not only coming from England, but Wales, Scotland and Ireland, and later from the more exotic parts of the world – Australia, Canada, New Zealand, to name but a few.

Grin-a-Lot, the Comedian, sent a postcard to Nod-a-Lot, then came a message on a card from Greet-a-Lot, the Hotel Receptionist, to be followed by Nora-a-Lot, the Gourmet, Stew-a-Lot, the Chef, Sue-a-Lot, the Solicitor and Ride-a-Lot, the Jockey. And there were more.

Almost three months had passed and the postcards kept coming. Whilst trying to retain a sense of humour about the whole business, I was aware that Yvonne was becoming uneasy, largely because the postcard writers knew so much about us.

It was almost as if someone was looking through the windows of our home, spying on our every movement.

We laid the cards out, sifting them so that those with similar handwriting were in batches. If we had hoped to find a pattern here we were disappointed, for cards with similar hand-writing were coming from different members of the Nod Dynasty and from varying parts of the country and, indeed, the world.

Roger – a very senior police officer in the Metropolitan Police Force, here in London Town, who sat with me amongst the tenors in St. Peter's Church Choir where we had a great deal of fun and made a quite superb job of the Easter Cantata – agreed to apply his not inconsiderable detective and forensic skills to the problem, but after an hour or so crouched down on our lounge carpet, Roger had to admit the Nod's family had beaten what was probably one of the finest and sharpest minds in the Met.

Disappeared!

It was at this point when I feared I might be losing my presence of mind – when Nod-a-Lot disappeared from his spot in the sun in our front garden. We had no warning.

One moment he was there. The next he had gone. We were devastated, shocked, gob-smacked, but perhaps a little relieved, too.

Days passed. The postman who, I would guess, had taken a peep or two at the messages on the postcards, grinned sheepishly as he walked steadfastly past our garden gate with nothing to deliver but bills, unwilling to admit that he had broken the post office code by reading our mail - if indeed he had done so and of that I cannot be certain.

It was in high summer that year when our good friend Brian and his charming wife, Linda, invited Yvonne, Graham, Heather, Richard and me to join them at their superbly appointed home on the outskirts of Braintree in North Essex for lunch one Saturday.

Now this was the kind of invitation you did not turn down, for Brian is a chef of considerable talent whilst Linda – the quieter of the two and the better looking – knows her way around the kitchen. Also joining us would be mutual friends Alan and Chris, with their sons, Paul and Neil – making a jolly party at which the wine would flow, enabling Yvonne and me to forget Garden Gnomes on one day at least (for whilst Nod-a-Lot had disappeared without trace, he was still in our thoughts having been part of our life for some time).

Pre-lunch drinks were enjoyed prior to settling down to eat. The main course followed the starter and as I tucked in there came a ring at the doorbell. For a reason which did not occur to me at the time – although it has to be said that by now I had imbibed a glass or two of excellent wine - I did not question when Brian and Linda suggested that I might go to the door to find out who had interrupted our meal.

Drawn up on the drive was a taxi cab with the rear door standing open and there on the seat sat – Nod-a-Lot! I was aghast and could barely speak as I lifted Nod-a-Lot from the cab, clasping him to my bosom and giving him a cuddle – as much as you can cuddle a plaster gnome. The driver smiled - as though he was the cat who had found the cream – when I asked him if there was anything to pay? He assured me that the journey was prepaid, driving off down the drive, chuckling as he went and no doubt rehearsing how he would explain this one to his pals in the pub that night.

Back at the lunch table, Brian, Linda and their guests – together with my family – were barely able to control their laughter. The project – for that is what it was – had been dreamed up by Linda and carried out with military precision by Brian and Linda's many friends and contacts around the country and the world. And it will go down in the annals of our family as the time that Ron was well and truly taken in, but it was not the first time, nor would it be the last.

The Fairy-in-Red

But the story has a sequel. It was our pleasure and delight in those days to throw a party for friends and neighbours around the New Year. As Nod-a-Lot had returned from his travels the previous summer, we were not surprised when a very attractive and very female Gnomess arrived at the party. Dressed seductively as the Fairy-in-Red, the young lady announced that she was Nod-a-Lot's fiancée, and demanded that she be fed fairy cakes – of which we had none because Yvonne had prepared a buffet supper with savouries in great variety, but no fairy cakes.

Furthermore the uninvited Fairy made clear to anyone who would listen that she and I had enjoyed a liaison of a somewhat lurid nature, making sure that Yvonne would hear what she had to say. Linda tells me that Yvonne's face was a picture as I tried to convince her that I had no knowledge of the young lady concerned, that I had never met her and that I did not know her, and if I did she was the last person in the world with whom I would wish to have any sort of liaison, let alone a lurid one.

Brian recalls that I was not just surprised at the arrival of the fairy – I was positively petrified!.

"You nearly died on the spot," Brian told me recently, *"and were zooming around like a thing demented."*

The Fairy was, in fact, Kay, Linda's daughter, who I had not met – before nor since, and more's the pity for she was a charming and shapely lass, to be sure.

We have a reminder of those New Year parties each time we walk in our garden where we now have two metal keg barrels, each fitted with a padded cushion top, covered with attractive waterproof material – the latter being purchased in Romford Market – and used as seats when it is warm where we may watch the passing of the seasons and listen to the tweeting of the birds. One year we awoke the morning after the New Year party to find that the paper-boy was having a problem reaching our front door for the garden path was filled with large (but empty) cardboard boxes marked clearly on the outside with the name of a famous brewer of beers, together with two metal keg barrels.

Brian, Alan and their cohorts in crime had departed from the party, but laid in wait until we had retired – and then dumped the rubbish in our garden to give the neighbours the impression that Yvonne and I had hosted a drunken orgy – or worse (or better, depending on how you view these things).

A few days later, Brian telephoned to arrange a date when he might call to collect the two keg barrels, but he was disappointed if he thought he could get away with that one for we had painted both with the very best Dulux Gloss and fitted cushions on top.

I believe that Brian found himself having to pay a deposit on the barrels non-return.

Brian, Linda, Alan, Chris and the gang enlivened many a New Year party. Held one year on the Eighth Day of Christmas, they arrived as Eight Maids-a-Milking - complete with pantomime cow.

Another party was held on the Eleventh Day of Christmas – when they marched up Aldborough Road North led by a Scots Piper in full dress with kilt and bagpipes. Fortunately we invited most of the neighbours to our parties.

Perhaps those who did not attend closed their curtains and turned the volume up on the TV.

At one time the gang inserted small gnome cards in a few hundred of my books on the shelves throughout the house – for years afterwards I would find a gnome card dropped from a book I took down to read.

Sense of humour

Graham, Heather and Richard – all young at the time – seemed to enjoy our New Year parties as they were allowed to stay up till late. It could hardly have been otherwise, for in our small house they would not have gone to sleep with some fifty people milling around.

When Richard was very small he sat beside Alan on the staircase to eat his plateful of food for supper. Alan enjoyed his food and drink, and had something of a paunch to prove it.

Looking up at Alan with the innocence of a five-year-old, Richard asked: *"Uncle Alan, if I eat up all my dinner will I have a fat tummy like you when I grow up?"* Fortunately, Alan had a sense of humour.

And while I am telling stories about Richard when he was small, I thought he looked extra pleased when at his third Christmas, Father Christmas brought him a torch.

The next time carrots were about to be served up for a meal, Richard announced that he did not have to eat those any more as he now had a torch and could see in the dark.

On one occasion Yvonne and I travelled with Graham, Heather and Richard to Brian's home. We went by train to Chelmsford where Brian met us in his luxurious Jaguar.

We were within a mile or so of Brian's home when we found ourselves driving on single track country lanes across windswept fields with not a house or cottage in sight.

Suddenly the car developed an alarming grinding noise - one of the tyres had a puncture and blew out, and before you could say *"Mine's a gin and tonic,"* we were driving on the metal wheel rims. Rather than call the RAC or the AA to sort things, Brian drove ever onwards for he did not wish to be late for lunch. It was an unnerving mile or so.

Talking with Brian more recently, he denies that he ever drove a Jag on a rim, but Yvonne confirms my recollection of the event. Whilst I am not taking sides in this, Yvonne's version makes the better story.

On arrival at Brian's home, we were somewhat taken aback to see that all his other guests were digging furiously with forks and spades in his large garden. All were suitably attired in old clothes whilst our family had dressed in the sort of smart gear that you would expect to wear if you are invited to lunch at a country house.

"The invitation did state that this was a garden(ing) party," said Brian, as we stood there in embarrassment, watching our fellow guests toiling under the hot sun – but, as usual, it was a wind-up and I fell for it!

Uncle Brian's water!
One Saturday in the 1970s, Brian and Linda invited us to lunch. They were generous hosts with a sideboard that groaned under the weight of good beers, wines and spirits. Richard, who was a toddler at the time, was thirsty on arrival and Yvonne asked Brian if she might have some cold water for him to drink.

"Sure, help yourself," said Brian, pointing to the sideboard.

Taking a tumbler, Yvonne poured a full glass of water, passing it to Richard who – being thirsty from the journey – took a big swig, gulping it down in one go. Perhaps ten seconds passed before Richard let out a mighty cry, yelling at the top of his voice that he *"did not like Uncle Brian's water!"*

Not surprising, for Yvonne had assumed that the colourless liquid in all the jugs on the sideboard would be water, but the one she chose was filled with neat gin!

Richard dropped off to sleep shortly afterwards, waking some twelve hours later none the worse for wear. He drinks whiskey these days, with expensive tastes for he has a preference for a twelve-year single malt – either Auchentoshan or Bowmore Enigma.

Heather was off to Girl Guide camp the following weekend and needed to collect dead branches to build camp gadgets. The woods near Brian's home were ideal for this – and Heather spent most of the afternoon deep in those woods with Neil, who was her age and who had taken a shine to her. It was said (by his mother) that Neil had two photographs by his bed – one of Her Majesty The Queen and the other of my daughter, Heather Lee!

The Scouts amongst us were amused to note from the gear list that Heather had been given by the Girl Guides that she was to take string – but not of the hairy variety, by which we assume they meant sisal.

How the traffic lights came to Aldborough Road

If you were to stand today where the A12 intersects with Aldborough Road – both North and South – here in sunny Aldborough Hatch (in the London Borough of Redbridge with a postal address which continues to claim, somewhat perversely, that we remain part of the County of Essex) you would be hard put to imagine that only a mere forty or so years ago there were no traffic lights at this busy junction.

In those halcyon days cars, lorries, bicycles, motor cycles and the occasional horse-drawn vehicle would approach the junction from the North, South, East or West, giving way to each other, with a wave of the hand and, sometimes, the exchange of a few pleasantries about the weather before going merrily on their journey.

Traffic went about its daily business in what might be termed a very gentlemanly (or ladylike) and somewhat refined manner.

Indeed, two cars passing each other would sometimes stop as their drivers wound down their windows to pass the time of day or to exchange the latest gossip. It had been thus for more years than most of us could imagine and, I would guess, few of us at that time thought that anything would change.

Rumbling

But in the early 1960s, there was a rumbling in the air. As post-war austerity receded, more and more vehicles were using the A12 and – would you believe it - a few of these wanted to turn left or right into Aldborough Road North or South.

To make matters worse, some drivers travelling from the East would decide that they wished to turn into Aldborough Road North, moving across the lines of traffic that were jogging out from London in the West. And if simultaneously – and at the same time – a driver journeying from the West made the decision to turn into Aldborough Road South, a confrontation of sorts would occur. And that could be painful.

At first there were no problems. Vehicles were few. Traffic jams did not occur. Juggernauts were only just beginning to make an appearance on the roads of this Emerald Isle.

But over a year or two the volume of traffic increased and speed became the norm. So much so that accidents occurred with grim regularity at that junction with results that were declared disastrous by many residents and especially so by those folk who found themselves lifted high into the air by a vehicle only to be dumped unceremoniously over the brick wall surrounding Aldborough Court, the post-war block on flats at the North East corner of the junction.

Farmer Peter from Aldborough Hall Farm made regular trips to the London markets in the early morning and, having successfully crossed over the lane of traffic travelling eastwards towards the Continent of Europe via Harwich, would find himself stuck in the middle of the dual carriageway, waiting for a break in the westbound flow so that he, too, could make his way into London.

But Peter's dilemma was whether it was best to allow the front of his vehicle to stick out into the westbound traffic or to leave the rear jutting into the traffic going east. On at least two occasions he did the latter – only to have vehicles running into him, which was painful to say the least.

The brick wall surrounding Aldborough Court took many a hard blow from a vehicle. Indeed, cars and lorries were careering through the wall time after time, for hardly had the Council's bricklayers made good the damage, when another driver decided to see how big a dent he could make in the brickwork.

"No, no, no!"

Attempts had been made to encourage the Department of Transport to install traffic lights.

"No, no, no," declared the Men from the Ministry, *"the volume of traffic at the junction does not warrant this."*

"Yes, yes, yes," replied the inhabitants of Aldborough Hatch, *"for we have seen with our very own eyes the bricks flying from the wall at Aldborough Court."*

But the Men from the Ministry were unmoved and even made public the results of a survey said to have been carried out by their Department.

"Ho, ho, ho!" cried the inhabitants of Aldborough Hatch – as one man and one woman – for the figures were laughable, bearing no resemblance to what we knew were the true facts.

"Something must be done," affirmed many but, as so often happens on these occasions, those who called for action then retired quietly behind their front doors to sit in their armchairs in the hope that someone else would rise off their rear ends to get things moving.

It so happened that at that time I was Scout Leader of the 1st Aldborough Hatch (St. Peter's) Scout Group and, noting that there was concern within the local community, and after deep and meaningful discussion with my fellow leaders within the Scout Group, we set about disproving the Men from the Ministry.

We chose a Friday and arranged for one Scout and one adult to man every junction between Barley Lane (in the East) and the Green Gate (in the West) – a distance of almost a mile - from 6am to 9am and again from 4pm to 7pm – the two periods of major rush hour.

We compiled our statistics and noting that they made the Department's figures look like a fairy tale or a figment of the Man from the Ministry's imagination (assuming that such a thing existed, of which I had grave doubts at the time), we sent off our results.

The response was – not surprisingly - condescending in the extreme, implying that account could not possibly be taken of a survey carried out by Scouts – even if their parents and other adults were in attendance.

"Whatever next!" exclaimed not just the Man from the Ministry, but all his fellow Men from the Ministry, too. We were livid – and made our views well known in the local press. That set the cat amongst the pigeons, I can tell you, as local politicians leapt onto our bandwagon – for there must have been an election in the offing.

Our voice from the wilderness of Aldborough Hatch was heard finally in Whitehall – or wherever the Men from the Ministry were hanging out at the time - and within a matter of months, workmen appeared and holes were dug as brand new traffic lights were installed. And they are there to this day.

So next time you pause at red at the A12, waiting to move off when the lights turn to green, just remember that the installation of traffic lights at this junction owes its origin to the 1st Aldborough Hatch (St. Peter's) Scout Group. And that's a fact.

But if the traffic jam extends up Aldborough Road North and past the Dick Turpin, please don't call me!

It's not my fault and, in any case, I do not drive!

The night I was driven to Gilwell Park for a sauna

Tony, who had been reading *Just an Essex Lad* (a book, incidentally, which you should read if you have not done so already, but which is now sadly out of print, although it could be reprinted if there was sufficient call for this), reminded me that I have omitted from the book the story of my escapade with an Arab in the late 1960s. And so here it is.

The new Sauna at Gilwell Park, the Scout Association's Adult Leader Training Centre in Chingford, Essex, was to be officially commissioned and I had been invited to take one of the first saunas in my role as Editor of SCOUTING. Tony, a colleague who was Assistant Director of Leader Training, with special responsibility for Venture Scouts at Gilwell, had kindly offered to drive me by car. Yvonne was out on some errand of mercy or other when Tony called.

Auntie Una, who was baby-sitting the infant Graham and Heather, was unaware of the fact that I would be travelling with Tony to Gilwell, but Auntie Una opened the front door to be confronted by Tony – in full Arab dress. Dashing out to the car – for we were running behind time – I called to Una to tell Yvonne that I would not be late. Una was totally taken aback at the fact that I had disappeared into the night with an Arab – and awaited Yvonne's return with some anxiety, telling her that I had in all probability, and almost certainly, been kidnapped and would never be seen alive again.

Abuse

During the journey Tony stopped the car at a red traffic light and as he did so a driver pulled up on Tony's side, winding down the window to indicate that he wished to speak with Tony.

Being a kindly sort and ever wishing to be helpful, Tony wound his window down at which the driver in the other car called out: *"B****y W*g!"* wound his window up and drove off at speed.

In that split second Tony and I realised with a jolt what it must be like to be subjected to racial abuse.

Prior to the day, John, the Director of Leader Training at Gilwell Park, had called me on the telephone to explain in the condescending manner he used when addressing the lower orders (of which I was surely one in his mind) that I might not have appreciated the fact that a sauna is taken in the nude.

I had responded that nude bathing was against my religion, but poor John continued to insist that I should be nude, whilst I protested that this was impossible. With the comment that he would speak with me when I arrived at Gilwell, we ended our telephone revelry.

John was waiting for me as I walked from the changing rooms – to find that I was, indeed, nude but wearing a set of Wolf Fangs hanging on a leather thong around my neck.

This set of Fangs was my highly treasured possession having been presented to me by John himself when he discovered that I had not undertaken a Scout Leader's Woodbadge Training Course for Adult Leaders – but one for Wolf Cub Leaders. In the early days of the Scout Movement, Wolf Cub Leaders were not awarded the beads of the Woodbadge, but were given a set of wolf fangs instead. John never really got over the fact that I had written a number of books and articles for the Scout Section, but my only training was as a Wolf Cub leader.

A plethora of Headquarters Commissioners

One of my former colleagues on the professional staff of The Scout Association has remarked that on reading *Just an Essex Lad* he was surprised that I made little mention of what he termed *"the plethora of Headquarters Commissioners with whom we had to deal in the 1970s"*.

This colleague had good reason to have strong feelings about some of the volunteers who made up the happy breed of HQ Commissioners in the 1970s for it was rumoured that a few of them had put the boot in as far as he was concerned – which resulted in his leaving the staff.

He remembers *"a certain Air Vice Marshall who on the day that the Committee of the Council had decided that I must go rushed up to me in Baden-Powell House to enquire after my health! This was only to be beaten by another HQ Commissioner who dashed into the Programme and Training Department a few days later - and before the bullet had been fired - to ask loudly: 'Is he still here?' - and I was!"*

That same colleague often assisted the Celebrant with the administration of Holy Communion at his local church back home. Holding a senior professional staff appointment with The Scout Association, he was present at a national conference in one of the large universities when he was invited by the Celebrant at Holy Communion to assist in similar fashion.

My colleague was robed for the service when the then Chief Executive Commissioner discovered that he was to do so – and banned him from so doing on the spurious basis that some of the volunteer leaders would not like it as he was a member of the professional staff. So much for Christian charity. What was even more odd was the fact that the Chief Executive Commissioner was himself a Lay Reader in the Church of England.

My personal experience with Headquarters Commissioners was less alarming, for unlike my colleagues involved with boy and adult training and programmes and the like, I did not have a Headquarters Commissioner for Editorial in my role as Editor of SCOUTING magazine (and that was a mighty relief, I can tell you!).

The Commissioners for Cub Scouts and Venture Scouts enjoyed writing, contributing to both the magazine and the Association's range of books. Both treated me with kindness, courtesy and a certain respect.

The one time that I was embarrassed by a Headquarters Commissioner for Scouts was when Lawrence Stringer appeared at my home on Boxing Day 1967 at around eleven in the morning.

Lawrence had taken the Occasional Court at Stratford as a magistrate and dropped in to leave a sheaf of proofs for *The Patrol Leader's Handbook* which I was writing. I was still in my pyjamas and dressing gown, playing with my eldest son who was then nearly four.

Lawrence strode in, dropped to his hands and knees, and pushed Graham up and down the hall in a truck the little boy had for Christmas. I was embarrassed but Lawrence – gentleman that he was – did not even comment (but I guess he made a mental note of the fact that I was unshaven at eleven in the morning on Boxing Day nonetheless!).

The Air Vice Marshall referred to earlier was, in fact, Ilford born and bred. Having served his country in the air, he took a liking to the water, living to the west of London on the banks of the River Thames. His home was on the south side of the river, but the means of travel into London was by train which necessitated his making his way to the north side – by rowing boat. This was fine when the weather was calm and balmy, but he found himself and his family often marooned when the rains and flood waters came.

(Above) The spire at St. Peter's Aldborough Hatch. The church was built from the stones of the old Westminster Bridge and consecrated in 1863.

A problem solved

Maintenance of St Peter's Church in Aldborough Hatch is something that we live with year in and year out. Hardly is one problem solved when another rears its head. Back in 1983 St. Peter's was 120-years-old and having recently installed a damp course, dealt with dry rot and protected the windows from the unwanted attention of vandals, we were faced with an urgent need to redecorate the interior of the church. Quotations for painting and filling in the cracks came to around £2,500.

With other equally urgent work waiting to be done, we simply did not have this kind of cash.

Was this a case for the involvement of the local Community Service (CS) Unit, whereby offenders were sentenced by the courts to carry out unpaid work in the community in reparation for their offending?

Our approach the CS organiser for North East London was received with a natural caution. Church halls and similar facilities used by a wide section of the community were regularly tackled, but CS had to be convinced that our church building served this purpose and that the church members themselves were prepared to roll up their sleeves – and were not merely seeking cheap labour.

At that time CS in North East London was used only as an alternative to a custodial sentence, and since the scheme began in 1975 the number of orders made each year has risen from 154 to something in excess of 600. Estimates of the cost of keeping a married man with a family in prison in 1983 were around £250 a week - probably more if the social security support for wife and children back home was taken into account. The cost per offender of operating a CS scheme was less than £20 a week.

After two site meetings - when hard questions were asked and answered - the project at St Peter's was given the go-ahead.

Local doubts and fears

The reaction from some members of the Parochial Church Council and in the local community to the news that the project could go forward was interesting - and, at times, slightly alarming.

I realised that my week-by-week involvement at the court as a magistrate gave me an appreciation of CS that was by no means shared by others locally.

Would they be unemployed youngsters?

Would they be unskilled?

Would they be supervised?

Would they knock our church about?

Some folk were convinced that offenders in arrowed-suits, carrying pickaxes aloft, would march up Aldborough Road North towards our church, grim-faced with chains clanking around ankles!

To those whose daily diet is the tabloid press, it was perhaps not surprising if it all smacked of 'soft options': of people who should be in prison lounging around in the pews, while trendy social workers tried to sort out what had gone wrong when they were babes-in-arms.

A problem that concerned many was that the CS Unit could not give a firm date for completion. With the after-effects of the lack of a proper damp course showing in the plaster, they would not know until they started how long re-plastering would take, nor how much plaster would be needed. They suggested we bought a bag or two: in the end we used 15 cwt in all!

At that time most CS took place on Saturdays or Sundays, but not on weekdays.

The reasons were obvious, for part of the idea behind a non-custodial sentence must be to allow the offender to continue to hold down a job, or to look for work if he or she is unemployed.

Today CS goes on all through the week, but back in 1983 our project would only operate on Sundays and services would be held in the church halls while the work was being carried out.

Inevitably, though, there were those who objected to the fact that their normal place of worship would be out of action for several months. A commercial contractor might have done a fill-and-paint job in a week or so, but at least three weeks would have been required for the sort of plastering and painting job the Unit tackled for us - and the longer time between each Sunday's working did at least allow the plaster to dry thoroughly before painting. In the event, a majority of the Parochial Church Council's twenty members voted in favour of the project: none voted against, but some abstained. Roger, an inspector in the Met (he who had applied his detective experience to the mystery of Nod-a-Lot's disappearance as recorded earlier), and I were appointed from the Church Council as co-ordinators - and, as we confided to each other with more than a little amusement, as scapegoats if the lads really did knock a hole through one of the walls!

Getting the project started

Each Sunday we rose by seven to set out the hall for church services – the first of which was scheduled for 8am. This involved putting out the chairs, setting up the altar and carrying the communion vessels, vestments, hymn and prayer books, and the like from the church to the hall. A very small group of church members did this – stumbling on the frosty grass in the dark in winter, but listening to bird song in the spring and summer.

At nine-thirty coffee and tea awaited the members of the Unit as they arrived - it was often bitterly cold and they travelled for distances of up to ten miles, usually on bikes or by public transport.

Roger and I were there for most of each Sunday, and we were joined by Martyn and Patrick, fellow magistrates, and other members of the congregation. We made hot drinks, washed-up, fetched materials when they were required, carried chairs into the packed hall where services were being held and generally were around to help.

On site we had two highly skilled Supervisors. Builders by profession, they were employed by the Unit at weekends. The success of our project relied heavily on both their technical skill and their ability to handle a mixed team whose ages ranged from seventeen to fifty-eight.

Part of the Probation Service's assessment, in its report to the court before a community service order was made, concerned the offender's physical fitness to carry out this type of work - and his or her willingness to do so – but specific skills could not be assumed. As it happened, two offenders working at St Peter's were trained plasterers and one was a roofer, who was used to scaling ladders at great height, but others without the skills required had to be taught.

Not only did this help with the work being undertaken, it was hoped that this training given on the job would provide offenders with additional skills that they could use in employment or in their own homes later.

From the start it was made clear that a professional job was the aim; merely filling in the visible cracks in the plaster and slapping a coat or two of paint on the walls was not what the Supervisors had in mind. Loose plaster was removed and new plaster applied - with a finish that many said was superior to the work carried out by the builders who handled the dry rot.

A sealant coat was applied to the walls first, followed by three coats of outdoor emulsion. Crumbling stonework in the windows was renovated.

From a paint-and-fill job costing perhaps £2,500, the project developed into something far more ambitious, something that would have cost well in excess of £5,000 - and the only financial outlay for St Peter's had been in providing the materials . . . less than £500.

With the task completed after four months, the word 'professional' was on the lips of everyone who had seen what had been achieved.

But there was one disappointment which, in fact, turned out to be a bonus.

Two-way involvement

In the early discussions with the Unit we had suggested that members of the church might work alongside the offenders.

Those of us in the church saw it as an opportunity to get to know the members of the Unit and to show that we were prepared to do our share of the work. But with an average attendance of ten members of the Unit each Sunday, there was a limit on how many could be involved in plastering and painting at any one time.

If we regretted that we were unable to work alongside the Unit, we found that our being there every Sunday did give us the chance to get to know them.

As for the members of the Unit, they clearly appreciated the fact that we did not merely open up the building and leave them to get on with it - something which happened, we learned afterwards, on many projects that the Unit tackled.

The bonus came during the Christmas break, when members of the church carried on with the painting, replaced rotting floorboards under one side of the choir stalls, and planned other improvements to be tackled in the months ahead.

Woodwork was renovated, electricity meters boxed in, wrought iron window sill supports repaired and repainted, and there were plans to renovate the pews.

With the help of a donation from a long-serving member of St. Peter's, we were able to rip out the fluorescent strip lights (which made the church feel even more stark and much colder on winter days) and to install a modern lighting system (that casts a warming glow). And the CS Unit acted as the spur to get these things done.

A growing relationship

Slowly but surely a relationship developed between the church and those in the Unit.

Quite how they found out that Roger was a policeman remains a mystery, but at coffee breaks the conversation would turn to his work in London's West End. Roger was not around on the Sunday following the tragic Harrods' bombing just before Christmas - and more than one member of the Unit asked, with obvious concern, if he had been on duty in Knightsbridge the previous day.

Someone who joined the Unit after a month or so recognised me from court - and for a week or two the conversation was stilted. Then, on a January morning, I boarded the London Underground and one station along the line that same man came into the carriage. He spotted the empty seat at my side, sat down, and we chatted all the way into London. But I doubt if we would have done so a month or two earlier.

We did not discuss the offences that had brought the men to the Unit, though we learned that those who cycled had often been sentenced for taking-and driving-away or for drink-driving offences and were, therefore, disqualified from driving.

Two seventeen-year-olds found out that they were both butchers and were soon engaged in animated conversation on the scaffolding about this cut and that joint. Two were keen Saturday afternoon rugby players and were among a small group who would start the day complaining about getting up early after a long evening's drinking.

For some of the younger offenders there might have been a little bravado - of the *"What were you done for?"* variety - when they first joined the Unit. But as the weeks went by they were more inclined to talk about the night out on Saturday or the job they were starting on Monday. One young man in his early twenties kept us informed about the progress he and a group of friends were making with fitting-out their soon-to-be-opened gymnasium and health centre.

Second thoughts

What of those in the local community and the church who had doubts when we started?

They watched and their confidence in the Unit grew week by week; to their credit, most were big enough to admit that they were wrong.

There was one Sunday morning early on when I feared that we might be in trouble with some members of the congregation. The Vicar had suggested that folk might wish to poke their heads around the church doors after morning service to see what was happening.

A number did so – just as three lads were removing the pulpit from its rostrum and half-a-dozen others were attacking crumbling plaster with hammers. Some urgent reassurance that their beloved church was not about to be totally destroyed was necessary!

Before the project started, fellow magistrates and friends in the probation service and the police had sounded well-intentioned warning notes. Some had experienced difficulties with CS or knew of others who had. If the success of the project at St Peter's relied heavily on the on-site supervisors, they would agree that it did not rest there.

On the final Sunday members of St. Peter's cooked lunch for everyone – a full roast with all the trimmings. With little fuss, we presented the Supervisors with framed prints of St Peter's. Their reaction was simply that the co-operation between the church and the Unit had been the key to the project's success. They felt welcome and their work appreciated.

Society tends to lock its problems away, out of sight. My view at that time – and it has not changed – was that if CS as an alternative to a custodial sentence was to work, the community that had been offended against should be prepared to be involved in that alternative. And with a re-offending rate well below thirty per cent at that time, CS must have had something going for it.

As a footnote, I quote from the *Redbridge Guardian*, one of our local newspapers. With the agreement of everyone involved, a reporter and photographer visited the site and spoke with a number of the offenders. One of them, who had been sentenced for driving whilst disqualified commented: *"It's such a lot of work and a lot of time taken away from me that I don't think I'll commit another offence. I don't want a prison sentence and that's what I'll get the next time."*

Smiles and tears

Looking back there were some amusing moments and others that stopped us in our tracks.

In the early 80s when this work was carried out, I was sitting in the local magistrates' court on a series of trials involving infringements of the Sunday Trading Laws – which then prohibited DIY stores opening on a Sunday. If the men ran out of plaster during a Sunday, we did not want to wait a week before we could continue with the work – and so Roger of the Met and me of the Court would drive off to a large DIY store to buy what was necessary! Noting that often the law is an ass, Roger and I merely smiled.

The oldest offender to work at St. Peter's was a sad man in his late fifties who had worked all his life for London Underground and had been ticket collector at a local station. He pleaded guilty to theft – pocketing excess fares – as the result of which he had lost his job and his pension. He was often tearful when he came to St. Peter's for the shame hurt him deeply. I often think of the tragedy that the man had brought upon himself when I look at the two light fittings on the West Wall at St. Peter's – for he had spent his time at St. Peter's rubbing down the metal work and painting it in black and gold.

A number of the offenders working at St. Peter's took great pride in their work. At the start of the project the hanging cross in the Chancel was taken to Aldborough Hall Farm, where Doreen and Lucy repainted it.

When the cross was re-hung, one of the offenders suggested that the arches over the windows should be painted in the same red and blue as the cross.

They experimented with one window and parishioners were asked to come into the church to make the decision as to whether or not all the window arches should receive similar treatment.

They decided that the colours enhanced the church – and the arches were painted.

Some months later the CS Unit returned to St. Peter's for a further three months or so. This time they worked in the church halls where, in addition to completely redecorating, they cut through from the Vestry into the Back Hall to make a doorway and broke through from the Large Hall to the Back Hall, fitting sliding doors in place.

I like to think that both projects were a great success.

Not a good idea!

Back in the days of yore members of St. Peter's Aldborough Hatch and their friends undertook the mammoth task of cutting the grass in the churchyard.

We were younger then and set about the task with great gusto. Indeed, so great was our gusto that we also clipped the hedges, often dressed in shorts and baring our chests to the heat of the sun, although this practice came to an abrupt halt one summer in the early 1980s when a particularly virile insect infected the hedge abutting onto Aldborough Road North.

Les and others were badly bitten, so much so that they had to take to their beds in darkened rooms, whilst the Men-From-The-Council arrived, dressed in the kind of suits you would expect to wear if a nuclear attack was imminent, carrying spray guns with which they attacked the insects. So successful were they that this variety of insect has not returned – *yet!*

In 1987 the Rev Michael Trodden arrived as our new Vicar. He watched the goings-on in the churchyard and, indeed, joined in, but it became very clear to him that the grass and hedge cutters were getting older by the year and were taking much longer to complete the work.

Indeed, hardly had they reached the far end of the churchyard, when they had to start all over again at the beginning where the grass was once again knee high.

Bright idea

In the following summer the Vicar had a bright idea. Up the road at the Aldborough Hall Equestrian Centre Bob and Mary had a flock of Jacob Sheep and sheep eat grass.

And so it came to pass that one warm summer evening in 1988 the Vicar led the Men of St. Peter's Choir and other volunteers up Aldborough Road North where they took command of a flock of Jacob Sheep – under the watchful eye of Bob and Mary - with the intention of driving them back down the road and into the churchyard.

Now you may know this – and yet you may not – but sheep tend to have a mind of their own and do not take too kindly to being herded by men who may make a passable attempt at singing alto, tenor, baritone or bass, but are not cut out to be shepherds.

All went well until we approached the Dick Turpin, our local hostelry (and nowadays an upmarket restaurant) when one sheep decided that the grass looked greener on the other side of the hedge leading onto Dickie Lewis's Aldborough Hatch Farm.

Diving through a gap in the hedge, the sheep found himself in a field of barley which was ripe for cutting.

Anxious not to miss out on anything, the rest of the flock followed, pursued by the Vicar and the Men of the Choir – much to the amusement of the patrons of the Dick Turpin who were not used to being entertained in this way whilst supping their ale.

Spectacle

Indeed, the spectacle of the worthy Vicar, crawling through a hedge in pursuit of 102 sheep, must have been astonishing to the denizens of the Dick Turpin, some of whom, no doubt, put down their glasses and hastily headed for home, swearing never to drink again.

With much arm waving, the flock was soon back on the road – only to find another gap in the hedge when the game of chase-me-through-the-barley-and-catch-me-if-you-can started all over again.

Eventually the churchyard was reached and the flock secured in a fenced off area, where they were left to eat as much grass as they could manage, whilst the Men of the Choir went joyfully to sing at choir practice and the Vicar went home to regale Mandy with the exploits of the evening.

Not surprisingly, the local press reported that the Vicar now had a new flock. *"People are quite used to seeing sheep in the country, but not in the heart of Redbridge,"* the Vicar told the *Ilford Recorder*. *"The sheep can get to places garden tools can't. It now makes it much easier to go round with the lawn mower."* Vowing to bring the 102-strong flock back when the grass got high again, the Vicar was photographed in the churchyard surrounded by sheep and holding a shepherd's crook.

(Above) Members of St. Peter's tend the flower beds in the Garden of Remembrance in the churchyard in 2010. These days we employ a gardener to keep the grass under control, but members of the church have regular workdays to tend the rose and flower beds, trim the trees along the church path and the hedges, and to keep things generally spick and span.

All was not well!

Whilst the local media may have painted a glowing picture of grass-munching sheep and a smiling Vicar, all was not well over the next few days. The sheep had, indeed, gorged themselves on the long grass, but they had also taken a fancy to the fresh flowers and bedding plants placed on graves by grieving relatives and friends. Furthermore, the sheep had become partial to the plastic flowers, the shrubs and anything else that happened to be thereabouts.

To make matters worse, the flock had decided that the church porch was a sheltered spot in which to sleep through the night – and had left evidence of their being there which, to put it mildly, was not pleasant to eye or nose. And further evidence of a similar kind was strewn on the pathways along which parishioners in their best Sunday clothes would be tripping for morning and evening services in a day or two.

The bride at a Saturday wedding had to pick her way up the path from the bridal car to the church porch through a splattering of droppings and a curious flock of sheep, some of whom took more than a passing interest in her floral bouquet and flowing veil.

Visitors wishing to visit the graves of their loved ones found their way barred by wire fencing. Having circumvented this, they were then fondly nuzzled by a sheep or three, some of whom were not averse to chomping away at a skirt or trousers if one looked more appetising than the grass of which they were soon tiring.

There was nothing for it. The flock had to return from whence it came and whilst profuse thanks were proffered to Bob and Mary, the Vicar made clear that some other means had to be found to manage the churchyard.

These days – and for some years past – the Parochial Church Council has employed a gardener to keep the grass under control. Members of St. Peter's, parishioners and those whose loved ones lie in the churchyard are invited to donate towards the cost and their support is much appreciated.

Throughout the year the Churchwardens organise a series of work days to carry out a range of maintenance in the churchyard – trimming the trees on the pathways to the porch, tending the gardens and carrying out a multitude of other tasks, but some of us are a bit wary of that hedge just in case those virile inspects decide to return.

The first gardener to be employed after the escapade with the Jacob Sheep was named – yes, it's a fact – Mr Bull!

Richard and the Great Storm

Yvonne and I had an undisturbed night's sleep on Thursday 15th October 1987, waking as usual at around six-thirty. I noticed that the wind was blowing hard as we made the morning cup of tea before waking fourteen-year-old Richard and sending him off to carry out his paper round.

The walk to Peter Woods' newsagent, tobacconist and confectioner's shop was a distance of a couple of hundred yards down Spearpoint Gardens and we were surprised when Richard returned a few minutes later.

Noting that he was white – nay, ashen - faced and somewhat confused, we asked what had brought him home? Taking my hand, Richard led me out from the front door – into what was clearly a howling gale of some considerable force.

Looking down the road, Richard pointed out a number of trees that had been uprooted and were laying across the roadway, explaining that no newspapers had been delivered to Mr Woods' emporium and that he was going back to bed.

Tuning in the radio, we discovered that an unusually strong weather system caused winds to hit much of Southern England and Northern France overnight – and we had slept through it all, due no doubt to the fact that we had a superb double glazing system installed a few years earlier.

Later we were to discover that it was the worst storm to hit England since the Great Storm of 1703 – 284 years earlier. Thousands of trees were uprooted across Southern England, whilst many buildings were severely damaged.

"Not my tree!"

Shortly after eight our neighbour, Mr Dunmore, knocked at our front door, to point out that he had an uprooted tree in his back garden. And indeed he had.

"It is not my tree," I explained, but this did not satisfy Mr Dunmore, who was of the opinion that the tree may well have come from another garden but as it has passed over my garden it became my responsibility.

Yvonne and I decided that this was not the time nor the place to argue about the ownership of an uprooted tree and, armed with a cross-saw, we climbed the fence into Mr Dunmore's garden to cut up the offending tree. Fortunately, it was a mere sapling so this did not take too long, but – ever concerned to make his point – Mr Dunmore insisted that we took all the timber into our garden and did not leave as much as a twig on his lawn. Later we discovered that the tree had come from Tom's garden next door to us but on the other side.

That morning Yvonne walked across the fields to Barkingside where she was working part-time, whilst I worked in my home office, having persuaded Richard that it was safe for him to journey by bus to school. Yvonne recalls that the Barnardo's office block in Tanner's Lane was undergoing maintenance, with scaffolding surrounding the building, and that an eerie sight greeted her with scaffold poles sticking out from the tiled roofs of the houses on the opposite side of the road.

The storm is, perhaps, best remembered for the frequently quoted comment by the BBC Weather Forecaster Michael Fish broadcast during the evening of 15th October – the night the storm hit - when he said: *"Earlier on today apparently a lady rang the BBC and said she heard that there was a hurricane on the way. Well don't worry if you're watching, there isn't."* However Michael wasn't talking about the UK at this point and was referring to a story in the News.

"My remarks referred to Florida and were a link to a news story about devastation in the Caribbean that had just been broadcast. The phone call was a member of staff reassuring his mother just before she set off there on holiday! I did broadcast saying 'batten down the hatches there's some really stormy weather on the way' - if the full clip was used all would be revealed."

"It's a miracle!"

Whenever we sing the hymn *Dear Lord and Father of mankind, forgive our foolish ways* in church I am reminded of the few days in February 1990 that

Yvonne and I spent with some thirty members of St. Peter's in the Holy Land, led by our Vicar, Rev Michael Trodden.

Apart from anything else, the trip will long be remembered for the fact that Derek commandeered a bus to take the party back to our hotel, that many of us ate far too many cream cakes and that some folk thought I had wrought a miracle out there in the Holy Land!

I wrote the following in the St. Peter's BROADSHEET for April that year.

Flying into Tel Aviv Airport in the early dawn, we drove on modern highways towards Jerusalem - to experience the conflicts of the old and the new City against a backcloth stretching to Biblical times. I had been warned that the holy sites might disappoint as they are today - and if they did, I looked at the sky, the olive groves and the barren hills and 2,000 years were swept away. Standing high on the Mount of Olives, looking past the Garden of Gethsemane and over the Kidron Valley to Jerusalem brought the Gospels to sparkling life. We were treading the ground where Jesus walked and talked. We followed the Via Dolorosa, the street along which Jesus carried his cross. It remains today a narrow, uphill, bustling thoroughfare filled with traders whose cries when they knew that we were British were different *("Fish and Chips three times a day, God save the Queen, Mrs. Thatcher! ")*, but whose raucous voices could have shouted *"Crucify, crucify!"* on that first Good Friday.

On Sunday morning, following our Service of Holy Communion, we walked the few steps from the chapel down onto the shore of the Sea of Galilee. The fishermen were putting out their nets. It was warm and the peacefulness seemingly swallowed us up. Centuries slipped by. *"O Sabbath rest by Galilee! O calm of hills above, where Jesus knelt to share with thee the silence of eternity."*

The contrast with Jerusalem was stark, for the beach was that peace we seek and so rarely find, whilst the street where Jesus carried His cross for us - with all its noise, laughter, grief, humour, tragedy - was the life He shared with us and gave for us.

My abiding memories of those fleeting days in the Holy Land are of the long-standing friendships that were bonded and of the new ones that were found; of our guide's deep knowledge of history and his gorgeous turn of phrase as he spoke of *"hiking cows"* and distances *"as the crow flows";* of Ruth's mouse and Lucy's flood; of Michael and Robin, our clergy who laughed with us at one moment and brought the Gospels into sharp focus the next; of cream cakes; of Martyn and Barbara on stage; of bodies floating on the Dead Sea and one that sat upright in terror; of Mandy, whose typically unselfish willingness to share Michael with us made it possible for our Vicar to lead; of the road from Jerusalem to Jericho; of the privilege that was ours that others from St. Peter's would have shared if their circumstances had permitted; and of the certain belief, that no one can take from me, that I stood where Jesus walked.

(Above) Fishermen on the Sea of Galilee in February 1990.

Miracle

An amusing incident occurred when we visited a kibbutz, where the two industries carried on were dairy farming and the manufacture of wheelchairs for the UK market.

I was editing MILK INDUSTRY magazine, the national magazine of the dairy industry, at the time and, naturally enough, I took an interest in the dairy side of things.

The herd of dairy cows was contained within a huge barn, each animal connected remotely to a computer which recorded distances walked each day and milk yield. These were not the 'hiking cows' referred to by our guide – which were free range on open hillsides and pastures.

Our guide - anxious to introduce me to the top man at the kibbutz as the dairy farming journalist from London – took me up a sharp incline where the top man was trying out one of the latest wheelchairs.

Following the introductions, I shook hands with the top man and stood talking for a few minutes, after which the top man rose from the wheelchair and walked into his office.

Picture the scene at the bottom of the hill where the members of our party were boarding the coach ready to leave the kibbutz. They looked up the hill, saw a man in a wheelchair, watched me placing my hand on his shoulder – and suddenly the man stood up and walked.

"It is a miracle," they cried!

On returning to the coach, the Vicar took me on one side and, with a broad smile, told me that he is the Vicar and if there are any miracles to be performed, he is the one to do them and not me!

"Where's yer ash tray, duck?"

For some thirty-five years Yvonne has been acting as Verger at weddings in St. Peter's Aldborough Hatch. It all started in 1975 when Rev Bill Barnes was Vicar. As the church could no longer afford to employ a live-in Verger and Caretaker, there was need for someone to clean the church and halls. Yvonne's mother had carried out the duties of church cleaner in a voluntary capacity in their home village of Aldringham in Suffolk and so it seemed natural enough for Yvonne to volunteer to do the same at St. Peter's.

And here we are, over three decades later, and Yvonne continues to pad up the road on Fridays or Saturdays to spend a happy hour dusting and hovering and polishing – tasks in which she is an acknowledged expert.

Indeed, it is said that if there were a University Course in Dusting, Hoovering and Polishing, Yvonne would pass out with a First Class Honours Degree – possibly with knobs on! Yvonne might, indeed, be the senior lecturer were there a dedicated faculty - or even the Principal!

In the early days of this voluntary duty, Yvonne was not supplied with a vacuum cleaner, but from time to time during the year would trudge up the road carting our machine. More recently vacuum cleaners have been provided – indeed she is now on her second Henry.

The role of church hall cleaner was taken on by another worthy soul, but it proved too much for a succession of volunteers and eventually the job became a paid post – which it is to this day. But Yvonne has stuck to the voluntary church cleaning like Superglue if you get it on your fingers (as I have done on numerous occasions).

One of the perks of being the voluntary church cleaner – and there are not many, for the work has to be done fifty-two weeks of the year in sunshine and rain, hailstorms and snow – is that Yvonne acts as Verger at weddings, for which she is paid a small honorarium.

In 1975 it amounted to the princely sum of a pound a wedding, but I gather it has gone up a bit since then.

Yvonne enjoys her work, setting out the hymn books or service sheets, giving a few words of advice to the ushers, comforting the bride and bridegroom's mothers, settling Aunt Nellie in a seat where she can watch the action unhindered and attending to the needs of Grandma which can be – and often are – many and varied.

It is fortunate that there are adequate toilet facilities close at hand in the church halls.

29

Yvonne gives photographers and those wielding video recorders very clear instructions so that they do not impede the progress of the service nor upset the solemnity of the occasion. Any creeping around on all fours, diving between the legs of the bridesmaids or hiding behind pillars is strictly forbidden.

Guests are treated with respect, except when they enter the church with a cigarette dangling from the corner of the mouth.

Yvonne recalls the occasion when she asked a guest to extinguish his cigarette as he walked through the church door.

His question: *"Where's yer ash tray, duck?"* received a prompt response from Yvonne of: *"We don't have ash trays in the House of God!"* – said, I would wager, with a somewhat disdainful tone of voice (at which Yvonne is an acknowledged expert when the need arises).

A major part of the Verger's duty at weddings is to ensure that the bridegroom is all sweetness and light, and in his rightful place, when the bride comes tripping up the church path on the arm of her doting father.

Furthermore, the Verger must be certain that the bride is in a right state of mind as she proceeds down the aisle. A liberal supply of tissues is required for this purpose and it also falls to the Verger to calm down any officiating Vicar of the male variety who may be overcome by a voluptuous bride, especially if the bride is showing more cleavage than is good for her.

Memorable

On one memorable Saturday afternoon three weddings took place one after the other at St. Peter's. At the start of the first wedding it was raining, but by the time the guests were arriving for the third wedding, a rainstorm to end all rainstorms was lashing the Hatch with gallons of wet and windy water.

There were a number of petite bridesmaids attending the bride in the final wedding of the afternoon. Had they walked from the cars in the roadway and up the church path they would have been soaked to the skin and as the churchyard was covered in six inches of water, they might have drowned into the bargain. Wedding cars drove up to the church porch, where bridesmaids were disgorged covered in a white sheet for the final few yards.

I received a telephone call at home in the late afternoon from Yvonne, asking me to help Churchwarden Derek who was attempting to open the drains in the churchyard so that the flood waters might subside.

Grabbing some old gardening clothes, I dashed up the road to find Derek - resplendent and immaculate in a two piece suit of the type that upmarket refuse operatives might wear – sweeping the water from the pathways and into the opened drains.

As we worked - sweeping and sloshing in the rainwater - two well-dressed and refined ladies passed by. With a sideways glance at Derek and me,

(Above) The church path at St. Peter's, which many a bride has walked.

one said to the other: *"It is excellent that the Council can get its workers out so quickly in an emergency!"*

Half-a-pack-of-Polo-Mints

Stephen in Wrexham, a teacher who wrote for me as a voluntary contributor to SCOUTING during my time as Editor in the 1970s, recalls working on the *Daily Squirrel* newspaper at Extoree, the International Camp for Handicapped Scouts at Gilwell Park in the early 1980s.

Stephen writes: *"Standing out among memories is the week of Extoree at Gilwell. A disco with half the participants in wheelchairs was one of the most hazardous Scout activities I have experienced.*

"At the end of the camp when the International Commissioners and Headquarters Commissioners for Extension Scouting were on the platform making thank-you speeches and receiving gifts, Jock Barr, Don Grisbrook, Derek Twine and I were standing right at the back of the gathering. One of the handicapped boys came slowly up to Jock and asked him why he was not up there getting a present after all he had done."

(Jock was, in fact, the volunteer organiser of this massive event and the man who should, by rights, have taken the credit for its success and would, without doubt, have taken all the criticism had it been a failure.)

"Jock made some excuse, the boy started to move away, then came back and gave Jock a half a roll of Polo Mints from his pocket and said: 'Here's a present for you.'

"My eyes filled with tears and with embarrassment I turned and faced into the adjacent bushes. Then I noticed the others were also standing with their backs to the gathering."

"I think my wife is dead"

Arthur (although this is not his name) lived up the road from here in a house which I pass on my way to St. Peter's.

Arthur's father built many of the houses around here in the 1930s, but Arthur was, as they say, a bit short of a shilling.

His first wife died young, having given Arthur two sons, who were lively lads. A year or so after the death of wife number one, Arthur married again.

One Sunday morning in the early 1990s, I was approaching St. Peter's at around ten on my way to the morning service when I spotted Arthur standing in his pyjamas at the garden gate.

Being a friendly fellow, I called to him a cheery *"Good morning"* as I trotted past, but Arthur leapt from behind his garden gate and stood in my path.

Looking me straight in the eye, he said: *"I would be grateful if you would please come inside for I think my wife is dead"*.

I went inside - missing Matins as a result, but as the psalm was rather long, I considered I had had a lucky escape.

"Where is your wife?" I asked Arthur.

"In bed," he said, and admitted under questioning that she may well have been dead for some hours.

"She was alive when she brought my cocoa upstairs," Arthur told me, *"which was just after ten last evening. But then I went to sleep and when I woke up about half an hour ago, I realised she was dead because she was stone cold and stiff."*

Not wishing to see Mrs Arthur stone cold and stiff, for the sight of Mrs Arthur hot and lithesome was too much for me to cope with under normal circumstances - I dialled 999.

Suffice to say that the police were kindness itself. I briefed them as they made their way down the garden path.

The police took a statement from me. Paramedics arrived.

Arthur, meanwhile, made tea and toast for everyone and suggested that if they wished to stay for lunch he would gladly provide the roast beef if they would be good enough to cook it.

I left at this point for I fear that had I not done so, Arthur might well have gone the way of his Good Second Wife!

The Weather Forecast for Aldborough Hatch

In the sixty of so years that I have been part of the community here in Aldborough Hatch, we have made our own entertainment in a myriad of ways – from the Scout *Gang Shows* to concerts in the church and church halls, and in school halls, too.

For many of these we wrote our own words, sometimes to music made famous by others. Perhaps one of the most unforgettable of these were the two versions written on the lines of the King Singers' *The weather forecast*.

The first was written in the 1980s, when folk like Mrs Chapman and Auntie Una Paul were hale and hearty – but I fear that the words have gone with them (and for all we know they could be singing them in heaven as a duet – and very fine it would sound, too, with Mrs Chapman taking the soprano line and Auntie Una the tenor).

The words of the 2003 version have been preserved and follow here. Whilst some of the folk mentioned may be strangers to many readers, I guess you will catch the drift of things nonetheless. They are set to the chants of Psalm 75 (W. H. Havergal) or Psalm 51 (M. Camidge). The chants are very well-known, but if you have difficulty in remembering how they go, please give me a ring – preferably during the hours of daylight.

Here is the / weather / forecast,
From to- / day un- / til tomorrow.
Flood waters are forecast for / Fairlop / Plain,
And will / swirl down / Aldborough Road / North.

Amanda Schlotter has / donned her / wellies,
To get / around / Aldborough Hatch / Farm.
Her winter wheat / is under / water,
And ducks are swimming / where the / corn should be.

Members of St / Peter's / Choir,
Have / climbed / up the / Bell Tower.
From here they watch / the waters / rise,
Singing hymns, chanting psalms, practising anthems,
          rehearsing canticles, and / eating / fish and / chips.

Churchwardens / Sue and / Roger,
Are maint- / aining an / air of / calm.
When the waters reach / the church / porch,
Sue will lie flat to keep the flood at bay, while / Roger will / ring the / Bishop.

Rabbi Maurice has / built him an / Ark,
Of / many / cubits in / length.
Traffic / on the / A12
Screeches to a halt / as he / turns into / Oaks Lane.

The Council / of the / Synagogue,
Are / praying / night and / day.
The sound / may be / heard,
As far / away as / Romford / Market.

Synagogue Secre- / tary Luc- / ille,
Has / taken / flood pre- / cautions.
Lucille has bought / herself / a boat,
And we would all be well-advised to take a /
        leaf / out of her / book.

Farmer Rudge is / all at / sea,
Surveying the scene / from the / roof of his / barn.
From there he / counts his / livestock.
Four sheep, two goats, two pot-bellied pigs, one donkey,
        thirty-four chickens, ten rabbits, a multitude of hamsters,
        and a ferret / who runs / up your / trousers.

Farmers' Wife Shirley Rudge is / all a / flutter,
It's an absolute / nightmare / she de- / clares,
Floating round the farmyard on a / home-made / raft,
Shirley has gathered all the stray cats and /
        dogs from / miles a- / round.

The Aldborough Hatch Defence Association / has been / mobilised,
And its / members / are ready / for action.
They have formed a / bucket / chain,
That stretches from Fairlop Plain in the North, to Seven Kings
        Park in the South, from Newbury Park Station in the West, to the
        nethermost regions of / Marks Gate / in the / East.

Val Smith has had her Mer / cedes con- / verted,
In- / to a / floating / home.
The rear seats / have been / removed,
To make space for essential foods, cream cakes,
        chocolate gateaux, jam doughnuts,
        and a / crate of / vintage / Chablis.

34

Bob Garrett at the / riding / stables,
Has gathered his flock of Jacob / sheep / safely / in.
But Bob is / all a / flutter
For Mary has / lost her / little / lamb.

Organist Bob has / played quite / splendidly,
We / think you / will a- / gree.
He plays with both / hands and / feet,
And occasionally, but not often, although more often that not,
        he gets the notes / in the / right / order.

That is the / weather / forecast
From / today / until / tomorrow.
But help is at hand so / do not / fear
To combat the flood we are selling wellie boots,
        mackintoshes, sandbags, sailing boats,
        all in aid of / Haven / House / Hospice.

Glory be to / Aldborough / Hatch,
And to / Newbury / Park as / well.
May the sun shine / for ever / more,
On Fairlop Plain, upon our farms, on our gardens, our window boxes,
        along the A12, and / upon / Newbury Park / station.

When the bells tinkled in the Hatch

If you happened to be in Aldborough Hatch during the summer months
from 1988 to 2005, you will have heard the soft, but pleasant, sound of
jingling bells for this was when St. Peter's boasted its very own home-
grown Morris Team. Fearful that the facts about this period of our history
will be lost in the mists of time, here – recorded for posterity - is the true
and unadulterated story of how it all began.
The Morris Men started when the lads of St. Peter's Choir and their male
pals took part in the International Cabaret at the St. Peter's Christmas Party
on Saturday 19th December 1987. Morris costumes were hastily run-up by
our lady wives and girl friends, and the laughter rang out as the Team
cavorted around the church halls beneath the mistletoe.
Such was the enjoyment of the audience that the decision was made to
form the St. Peter's Morris Men to perform at the Celebration Flower
Festival to mark 125 Years of our church at the end of June in the following
year. Cricket whites and shirts were purchased and floral bunches were
stitched to straw hats. Coloured scarves were procured in fetching shades
of blue and red, whilst the cross-over pieces (known within the business as

Baldrics) were made. Cecil Sharp House in London was contacted and the postman walked warily up Martyn's front garden path carrying a box of various sized bells that created a delightful cacophony of sound – but frightened the postman almost out of his wits. Staves were made from broom handles - we kept the manufacturers in business for many staves were broken across sore and bleeding knuckles in the weeks and years that followed. It has to be said that Brian was especially fierce where the staves were concerned, causing many injuries to himself and others – unintentionally, of course, but painful nonetheless.

A seasoned Morris Man and schoolteacher of our acquaintance gave us some rudimentary lessons and we were off. At first we danced to canned music played on a tape recorder, but later Martyn accompanied us on the piano accordion, playing first the white notes and then the black ones too.

First outing

At our first outing on the Green at St. Peter's on Saturday 25th June 1988, some members of the audience – recalling the amusement at the International Cabaret the previous Christmas – started to laugh, but one or two ladies of the Parish soon made it very clear that this was a serious business, warning that those who dared to laugh might find themselves struck down with a well-aimed and sharply pointed umbrella or high-heel.

And so it was that the St. Peter's Morris Men danced at each Flower Festival in the years that followed. The Men also undertook the occasional performance at Fêtes and such like outside the parish of St. Peter.

The very pinnacle of their prime was when they were invited by Mrs Joyce Harvey, JP, Bench Chairman at Redbridge Magistrates' Court, to perform at the Court Garden Party which was held that summer at the Chairman's home in Loughton, where Joyce lived with husband, John Harvey, formerly MP for Walthamstow East.

When the time came for the Morris Men to perform, the heavens opened and the rain came splashing down in a mighty torrent.

But Morris Men are made of sterner stuff and danced on the lawns, watched by the magistrates and their guests from inside the house – where they were dry, warm and cosy as they tucked into strawberries and cream.

All would have been well but for the fact that the lawns sloped away from the house, and the Morris Men moved slowly but surely into the far distance with each dance.

Music was canned on this occasion – and Yvonne was in charge of the tape recorder. A large umbrella was held over Yvonne by none other than John Hall JP – who was later elected as Bench Chairman, too.

Yvonne and John slid behind the Morris Men towards the vegetable garden, the raspberry canes and the strawberry beds.

The dancing over, the Morris Men were taken to a capacious garage where we dried off after a fashion whilst drinking wine and eating strawberries and cream.

Over the eighteen years the Morris Men became the Morris Team as ladies augmented the males. Three Vicars took part. The Rev Michael thumped us with a balloon on a stick, whilst the Reverends Tim and Clare took things more seriously as part of their fitness regimes.

For each Flower Festival the Team was resurrected, enhanced, dusted down and resuscitated.

Members came and went as bones began to ache and limbs stiffened, whilst others who could no longer hurl themselves around the greensward took to playing the drum and single jingle.

Home-grown

All the Team's dances were home-grown and based on the history of Aldborough Hatch – recalling the days when the Hatch was a village where rivalry existed on the farms of Fairlop Plain, when at the end of a hard day's hay-making in the fields, the young men of the village would fight for the favours of the young maidens as the sun went down. And for some of the Morris Team it has to be said that the sun went down on them a long time ago!

The St.Peter's Cudgels was a fertility dance and told the story of times of yore when the harvest was the big event of the year. The young men of the parish would wait until all was safely gathered in before pursuing the young maidens across the fields and into the haystacks. Sometimes there were more young men than nubile maidens - so they would fight with cudgels to decide which young man would take a young maiden to the Dick Turpin for a pie and a pint - before a frolic in the haystacks.

The Flamboynut Trunkles told the story of the final day of hay-making when the young men of the parish would chase the young maidens through the thick forest that covered Fairlop Plain up to the mid-19th Century. The maidens would run through the forest, pursued by the young men.

Often the young men would get lost, so they carried thick staves with them which they would throw to one another as they gambolled through the leafy glades. The staves they carried were known in the Village of Aldborough Hatch as Trunkles – but the derivation of that word is lost in history.

To impress the young maidens, the young men would dance in a flamboyant fashion, but – sadly – the scribe of the time could not spell flamboyant – and so it became known as the Flamboynut Trunkles.

Those who had the strength to do so lifted their Trunkles high in the air, but some allowed them to dangle. It was not a pretty sight.

The St. Peter's Threadle recalled the days of hay-making in Aldborough Hatch when – after a long day in the fields – the young men would be ready for an evening of jollification with the young maidens of the parish. But sometimes the young maidens would play hard to catch, as young maidens do – especially the nubile ones - and disappear into the forest.

The young men would set off in hot pursuit – but fearful that they might get lost in the dense undergrowth, the young men would clutch each others' scarf as they weaved and dived under the boughs of the trees.

The Dough-maker was a reminder that the inhabitants of Aldborough Hatch of yesteryear not only grew their own corn, but also turned that corn into bread. In this dance the four participants each represented an ingredient, which go to make the dough from which bread is made – flour, eggs, milk and yeast.

Their intricate meanderings illustrated how those four ingredients turned into a fine, crusty, scrumptious loaf.

Our Flower Festival theme in 2002 celebrated The Queen's Golden Jubilee and in recognition of The Queen's fifty years on the throne, the St. Peter's Morris Team presented a new dance - *Jubilee Japes* – dedicated to Her Majesty which had its roots in Victorian times.

Our Church of St. Peter was built from the stones of Westminster Bridge when Queen Victoria was on the throne.

The red and blue scarves represented two of the colours of our National Flag.

The white was missing, but such was the vigorous leaping required in the dance that the faces of the Team turned a whiter shade of pale as the dance neared its climax.

Variety

Singing was added at the turn of the Century – partly to bring some variety to the performance, but also to allow the older members of the Team to get their breath back after the exertions of the dance.

The repertoire was extensive – ranging from the raucous *Fling it here, Fling it there* to *Aldborough Hatch Fair* and *Daddy Fox*, from *All around my hat* to the tale of spurned love *Twas pleasant and delightful*.

Matthew, Mark, Luke and John was a three-part song filled to the brim with pathos which was known to bring tears to the eyes of those witnessing its rendition. We advised the audience to *"feel free to weep if you are moved to do so"*.

Written especially for the Flower Festival in 2002, the Morris Team's version of that famous ballad *O No John, No John, No John, No,* featured the then Deputy Prime Minister, the Rt Honourable John Prescott, MP, who was something of a local hero in these parts with many – for it was he who overturned the Planning Inspector's decision to allow the London City Racecourse to be built at Fairlop Waters to desecrate our beloved Fairlop Plain – which remains as Green Belt to this very day.

(Above) Fairlop Plain from Fairlop Waters, looking towards Hog Hill. Fairlop Plain featured in many of the tales regarding the derivation and history of the Morris Dances performed by the St. Peter's Morris Team.

Much lamented in their demise, the St. Peter's Morris Team's farewell performance took place at the Flower Festival in June 2005. Indeed, it is said that some folk cried for days on end at the news and refused to be comforted in their grief — well, Pat and Val did to be sure, although I doubt they will admit it.

The St. Peter's Morris Team will be remembered with affection by many, for the majority will mourn their going and the odd one or two who sighed with relief at their passing have wisely kept their heads down.

Banana sandwiches recalled

After some sixty years I made contact with Colin, a fellow student at Leyton County High School for Boys through Friends Reunited and Google on the internet. Reading *Just an Essex Lad* brought back memories for Colin, who was also able to put me straight on a few facts about our school-days. We both started at LCHS in 1944.

Colin and I travelled home together on the trolley bus to Leytonstone - he then caught the 148 to Goodmayes and I took the 66 to Newbury Park. He lives – and continues to live - in Goodmayes.

Unlike me, Colin stayed on to the Sixth Form for three years and gained an MA and BSc at University, teaching chemistry with posts as Head of Chemistry and Head of Science at local secondary schools. He joined the Redbridge Music Society when he was 16, went on the Committee at 17 and has been chairman for the past 30 years. I sent him a copy of my book and he has given me an excellent classical CD which he produced.

Colin remembers the treatment we received as first formers when the second and third formers captured us and put us in what they called 'The Black Hole'. But my memory of PE masters as recorded in *Just an Essex Lad* (which, as you may recall is my now out-of-print autobiography) appears to be somewhat out of kilter with the truth.

My namesake, Mr Jeffries, *"was not old, but quite a young man, possibly in his thirties,"* Colin recalls, *"but he did not last long and disappeared without warning, to be replaced by a man called Nicholas who was about 53. He was a kindly and sympathetic teacher, especially to those of us who had little talent for his subject."*

Colin recalls visiting my home during our school days. *"This was wartime and food was quite short and we were still on ration for many years after that. Of course, we had no bananas since they were not imported during the war. Did your mother make a banana spread using parsnips and banana essence? I seem to recall that this was a very successful experiment."* And he is right, it was, so much so that Mum's banana spread tasted better than real bananas!

Like me, Colin started in the B-stream but moved to the A-stream – I went up at the end of the first year. Miss Underwood, who was first to teach us French and was, I recall, something of a stunner, played cricket for the staff, bowling the School Captain, Vice-Captain and Cricket Captain out in a hat-trick. *"I do not think they were concentrating on the ball!"* comments Colin.

In the A-stream we had Mr Muswell for French, who made us sing the French vowel sounds at the start of every lesson. *"I remember that a naughty boy called Stephen (Tubby) Gaitley used to make silly sounds just to be difficult,"* said Colin, but I just recall that Gaitley had ginger hair and was what we would refer to as obese today, although we just called him fat.

"When I first started at LCHS there was a Maths teacher called Wolner-Bird who was very scruffy and many of the boys thought he was a cleaner," Colin recalls.

"In contrast there was the very dapper Chemistry teacher called 'Bud' Clark who retired in our first year. There was a Physics teacher called Berry, who was known as ' Wiggy' for obvious reasons. One of the teachers you may have remembered was called Lamb. He wrote a book called 'Chalk in My Hair' which was about LCHS. When asked whether it was about the school, Headmaster Dr Leonard Couch replied: 'Yes, but it was the product of a second class mind'."

Colin's memory for names is far better than mine. *"Maths was taught by Geoffrey Eustace Ryle – known to the boys as George – whilst Percy Cornelius Craven was the full name of the Latin master"* – we called him Percy to his face in the afternoons if it was clear that he has spent lunchtime at the Bakers' Arms.

"Arthur Cox was the terror of the German students. Then there was Victor Cohen, known as The Bear, who taught History and Economics. There was an English teacher called Fitzhugh who had a permanently flushed face."

My recollection of French School Certificate examinations is restricted to the oral where I was presented with an illustration of a farmyard. I stammered my way through a description which kept returning to the pig – for it was the only animal whose name I could remember in French.

Colin, however, recalls that after the written paper I told my friends about my translation of the French passage. It should have started with *"Agathe, the maid, was in the drawing room"* but I translated it as *"Agathe, the beautiful, was in the saloon".* As Colin remarked: *"With this picture in mind, the rest of the translation must have been quite difficult!"*

Colin also recalls that Frank (Billy) Rushton sometimes played the piano for us and that I found *La Fille aux Chevaux de Lin* was *"impressive".* I regret that my mind is a total blank in this regard.

Back to school – sixty years on

Apart from the initial burst of activity on Friends Reunited, things remained quiet on that front until I was informed that my old grammar school, Leyton County High School for Boys, would be holding a reunion for former pupils on Saturday 28th November 2010.

I made contact with two contemporaries, one of whom told me a bit about himself, whilst the other was pleased to know that I am still alive, read my book and continues to be in touch. I sent messages to a couple of others listed who were at the school with me, but they have not replied and could be snoozing down here or up there (depending on whether they are alive or not).

The occasion was the 80th Anniversary of opening of the school. The message from Paul Estcourt, who hosted the event, read: *"As I can't email everyone individually, I am sending further details to all. Apologies to those who cannot or do not wish to attend. There is no need to respond to me. I have today received further details from the college: '......the format of the day is quite informal - essentially an open day on Saturday 28th November starting at 1pm. We will have an exhibition in the main hall comprising many of the old photos and other documents from the College's archive. There will also be a chance to have a guided tour to see how the place has changed over the years. An article will appear in tomorrow's local Guardian'."*

An article did indeed appear in the *Wanstead and Woodford Guardian,* giving some of the school's history, first as a grammar school and nowadays as a Sixth Form College. Students at the school between 1920 and 1970 were invited, which meant there could be a goodly number of zimmer frames, sticks, mobility cars and the like.

It would appear that our host left the school in 1964, so is a mere youngster. I noted that amongst the former pupils listed as having agreed to attend were Trevor William Fosh (1970), Geoff Heaford (1959), Keith Lewis (1962), Kenny Miller (1960), David Tozer (1960) and Rob Tunbridge (1966) – plus me, of course, and as I departed from the school in 1949, I would appear to have been the oldest who had registered his intention of attending up to a couple of weeks in advance. I hoped I would be treated with all due deference.

I delved into some of the history of the school. Leyton County High School for Boys was formed in 1916 by amalgamation of Leyton and Leytonstone high schools. The school occupied temporary premises at Connaught Road until 1929, when it moved to new buildings in Essex Road. The opening was performed by the Prince of Wales. It was a selective grammar school for boys aged 11 to 18.

Leyton County High School for Girls was on Colworth Road, half a mile or so away, but to all intents and purposes as far as we boys were concerned when I was at school for it might as well have been on the other side of the moon. Any attempts at fraternisation were put down with an iron fist.

In 1968, Waltham Forest adopted the comprehensive system and in its new guise the school catered for mixed-ability 14 to 18-year-olds as Leyton Senior High School for Boys before a re-organisation in 1985 led a change of role as a co-educational sixth form college.

It now offers 33 A-Level subjects, and, as of 2008, 99% of the students passed their A-Levels. The school has formal partnerships with Queen Mary, University of London and the University of Westminster.

Famous

When I joined the school in 1944 the Headmaster was Dr Leonard Couch, nephew of Quiller-Couch (Q), the author. He was an austere and distant head – and I cannot recall ever speaking to him or being spoken to by him.

Amongst the famous former students are Frank Muir, Sir Derek Jacobi, Bobby Crush and Jonathan Ross (who, according to *The Guardian*, was earning £6M a year with the BBC until they parted company – only beaten narrowly by Her Majesty The Queen, whose £7M plus cash comes from the taxpayer as opposed to the TV Licence fund. Not that I begrudge my former school colleague his dosh – much!).

Michael McStay was a contemporary of mine, sitting in the same classroom and eating the same school dinner of watery cabbage, lukewarm meat and powdery mashed potatoes, following by semolina pudding that could have done with a dash more milk.

Michael's TV and film career took him into drama productions including the *Inspector Lynley Mysteries, No hiding place, Dr Who* and *The Sweeney.* I gather he now lives in the New Forest.

Amongst the more recent famous former students is footballer Lomana LuaLua, who was born in Zaire in 1980, but moved to the United Kingdom as a young boy in 1989. His family settled in Forest Gate where he started to play football at the age of 16. He was playing for Leyton Sixth Form College, where he studied performing arts, when he was spotted at the age of 17 by Third Division Colchester United. I'll bet you did not know that – and neither did I.

Anniversary

I attended the 80th Anniversary shin-dig. It was the building's 80th birthday that we were celebrating and I was gratified to see that a jolly crowd had assembled of the young, the not-so-young, the middle aged, the elderly, the old, the very old - and the folk that you took one look at and wondered how they had managed to get out of bed let alone make their way unaided to this event. And then you discovered that they were younger than you!

The London Borough of Waltham Forest's Leyton Sixth Form College offers a range of courses to nearly 2,000 students aged from sixteen to eighteen. The premises are vast for, in addition to massive restructuring within the walls of the original 1929 building, there is new build that has taken place over the twenty-four years since the co-educational sixth form college was formed in 1985. Now massive cranes and earth moving equipment are at work on what remains of most of the playing fields where state-of-the-art lecture halls, study rooms and studios will rise – covering with concrete the hallowed turf where cricket and football were played by the elite, whilst the rest of us had to walk to Leyton High Road for cricket on the Essex County Ground or Eton Manor on the Hackney Marshes for football.

Within the original building the cold stone floors have been replaced with warm carpeting, the bare red brick walls have been plastered and painted in bright colours. All windows are double glazed – gone are the metal window frames and single panes of glass. Corridors are no longer continuous, where the cold winds whistled in the winter and the heat in the summer made scraggy boys wilt.

Today the corridors are broken with swing doors in some places and widened in others, with small and larger rooms here, there and everywhere, and even over there, too.

From what I could see, the buildings offer first class facilities for teaching and learning. The College is superbly well equipped with the very latest technology and enough computers to keep everyone happy. The students I met were polite and intelligent, and the staff motivated and keen to demonstrate that this is the place to be if you are sixteen to eighteen and willing to learn.

Everyone was welcoming – from the security guard at the front door (who probably wondered how many more old fogies would be coming out of the woodwork, but was too kindly and well-mannered to say so) to a gentleman I took to be the Principal, for he moved forward to shake my hand, commenting that he was pleased to see me (and by the smile on his face, I believe he was).

Alone and outside

Whilst I rejoiced in all I saw and heard, I left the celebrations to stand - alone and outside - for a few minutes on the tarmac covered playground I first saw in September 1944 and last crossed in March 1950. A wave of immense sadness welled up inside as I stared up at the red bricks walls, untouched except by the ravages of wind, rain and sun over nearly sixty years.

For this was – to me and ever will be – Leyton County High School for Boys, the grammar school where I spent my formative boyhood at the end of the Second World War and during the austerity years that followed.

I came here as a skinny eleven-year-old who stammered, whose legs resembled bean stalks and whose ribs stood out – so much so that my nickname was Belson Bill, for in spite of my mother's daily ministering of cod liver oil and malt by the tablespoonful, my body bore some similarity to the poor wretches who were being rescued from the Nazi concentration camps at that time. I left five years later, still stammering, but healthier and with an education that was probably rudimentary by today's standards, but which enabled me to build on its foundations as I progressed through life – and for that I am grateful.

For a fleeting moment – out there in the windswept playground - it was playtime. In the fading light of a winter's afternoon strode Morgan, the Pownall Twins, Timms, Groom, McStay, Sicely, Venis, Bradbury, Herring, Pryke, Lay, Gaitley, Timcke. Music Master Mr Rushton cycled by and the baker's man rode in on his tricycle, selling warm buns at a penny from the box on the front – and then they were gone into the shadows.

I shivered as the wind blew.

The memory spun before me and passed as quickly as it came.

Where are they today?

Did they all achieve the promise they showed as boys and young men? How many are alive? Will I ever know?

I had travelled that day – as I did all those years ago – on the 66 bus from Newbury Park to Leytonstone, but the driver told us that he would not be going further than Wanstead Station.

Here I changed to a 145 which whisked me past The Green Man (now O'Neill's) and on to Leytonstone Station – for the 661 Trolley Buses no longer glide silently from the Green Man down Whipps Cross Road, past the hospital of that name to Essex Road and the Baker's Arms beyond.

At the station I caught a W15 low decker, alighting where James Lane met Essex Road – and walked the last two hundred yards until the familiar red bricks walls with iron railings and the red brick façade hove into view, both little changed over sixty years.

Back inside and in the main hall, I spotted John in what was the balcony, now blocked in to house a battery of lighting, projection and sound controls. John was at the school a year or so after me. Today we work closely together as chairmen of local residents' associations in Redbridge. Tagging onto a tour, we found ourselves in the company of a personable young lady, who seemed happy enough to indulge John and me in our nostalgic ramblings and rumblings.

Geography room no more

Mrs Cattell-Jones' geography room, upstairs in the far corner, is now divided into three small seminar rooms. Katy Bones, we called her, but she was specially kind to me, encouraging me to develop my talent to draw maps with accuracy and precision. In my day we looked out from Katy's classroom over green playing fields towards the towers of Whipps Cross Hospital on the horizon. The hospital – much expanded – is still there but the playing fields are no more - covered with completed and half-finished buildings.

Access upstairs along the back of the school is no longer via a corridor, which has been widened with small and larger rooms added. The gymnasium – with its wall bars from which we hung in agony - and cold showers - of dreaded memory - are gone. The stage in the main hall has been blocked off, for performances are now on the flat in a hall where the walls and ceilings are painted stark black - the boards with the names of Head Boys and Successful Students were removed at a time of political correctness in the 1980s when such things, I was told, were considered inappropriate and elitist.

It was on that stage where the likes of Sir Derek Jacobi and Michael McStay performed as fledgling actors - and on which Jonathan Ross might well have strutted - and under which many a boy had his first puff at an illicit cigarette, although much of this clandestine activity took place behind the bicycle sheds. Being a boys' only school nothing much else took place behind those bicycle sheds – well, nothing of which I was aware anyway.

45

Here in the main hall memorabilia stretching back to a time before I was born was on display.

In the main hall I met another John, who was part of the St. Peter's Aldborough Hatch crowd of my youth. John's sister, Pat, continues to live in the Hatch and I have kept in touch with John, who left the school in 1955. The two Johns and a friend of the first John who had travelled from Bournemouth for the day, trotted off to the Refectory to have tea and cakes, whilst I sought out a member of staff responsible for organising the event.

I presented her with a copy of *Just an Essex Lad* (my autobiography, but you knew that, didn't you?) and some printouts of the chapters covering my years at LCHS. Promising to read the book herself before placing it in the College library, the lady led me into what was once the Headmaster's study and where I had stammered my way through an interview in 1944 for selection. Here three media students made a video recording of a one-sided interview in which I did all the talking as they looked on wide-eyed.

Taking tea and avoiding the wide selection of tempting cakes in the Refectory, I realised that this was the Music Room in my time where Mr Rushton would play the piano and gramophone records to what must have seemed to him an often unappreciative audience.

Thundering havoc

Further down the corridor was the cloakroom with its rows of metal pegs on metal frames, where brick walls built outside and close to the windows protected us from the blast and flying glass of wartime's falling bombs. Here we sat beneath the metal pegs in the closing months of 1944 as Nazi doodlebugs zoomed overhead and flying-bombs and land-mines thundered down to wreak further havoc on the East End of London.

We could not find our way to Arty Young's Art Room above, nor to the Science Labs that filled the rest of the side corridor.

Do they still have those delicate brass scales in mahogany cases in the physics lab and are dead frogs dissected these days by those studying biology? I guess not.

In my day the Headmaster had a Secretary, we had a Deputy Headmaster and, perhaps, twenty-five or so teachers. That was the staff. Today's High Schools are staffed with Head Teachers, Deputies and Assistants, Heads of Teaching Departments, Year Heads, Teachers and a whole phalanx of support staff and folk beavering away in offices. We had a caretaker, living with his family on the premises, and cleaners who came in each evening – and I guess this is much the same nowadays. But teaching and learning have advanced – as they rightly should – and I would hazard a guess that a stammering skinny boy these days would soon be sorted out by one or other of the team!

(Top) Leyton County High School for Boys in Essex Road (on the left) with the main pitched roof assembly hall and two quadrangles on either side, and playing fields at the rear as I knew it in the 1940s. (Above) The central staircase today at what was Leyton County High School for Boys. In my day only 6th Formers and Staff were permitted to cross the hallway or climb those stairs – the rest of us had to trudge right round the building to reach classrooms on the other side.

47

Perhaps it was enough that today and yesterday's students and staff were milling around in the area behind the imposing front doors and outside what was the Headmaster's Office and below the two staircases that rose majestically to the floor above – an area that we boys of the 1940s were not permitted to cross on pain of the severest punishment LCHS could impose. I hoped that the library at the top of those never-to-be-climbed staircases would be a haven where I might reminisce, but it was not to be for the library is – yes, you have guessed - yet another seminar room.

One thing we did not have were the security guards who were very much in evidence during my visit. All were pleasant and helpful, but the fact that they needed to be employed full-time and were there at all is sad.

A friend engaged a security guard in conversation about the change in the ethnic make-up of the students today when compared with the early 1950s when he was around.

Then there was not a black face to be seen, said John, which worried me a little for the guard to whom we were talking told us that he came from Nigeria, but he smiled and was interested to hear that my son-in-law is from the Caribbean and I have two mixed race grandsons. I think all this came as something of a shock to my friend, but never mind.

(Above) The front of Leyton County High School for Boys as I remember it. I walked up the steps to the main door one September morning in 1944 – my first day – and not again until some 66 years later in 2009. The library stretched between classrooms on the first floor above the main doors – today it is a seminar room.

48

The Day when Uncle Mac presented the prizes

Some time before the 80th Anniversary celebrations referred to in the last chapter, I had made contact with my former Leyton County High School classmate, Brian, through the Friends Reunited website. Uncertain if I was the boy he knew, Brian remembered *"a lad called Jeffreys who had a wooden suitcase for a satchel."* Brian said that he had plenty of mementoes from his years at LCHS. He spent most of his working life in Rhodesia, leaving just before Mr. Mugabe took over. We corresponded briefly on Facebook.

Standing in the main hall at the celebrations, a tall man accompanied by his wife moved towards me, smiling in welcome. It was Brian and after a few pleasantries what turned out to be the highlight of the afternoon occurred, for Brian had very thoughtfully brought with him photocopies of some of those mementoes he had mentioned. But first he showed me the one photograph he had of some of our classmates in the football team. A young fresh-faced grinning Brian sat in the centre front – and I recognised him instantly and Mr Paine, the sports' teacher standing at the rear.

The first photocopy was of the Report for Form 1B at the Spring Term 1945.

Pupils were listed in the order in which they came in class starting at the top with three names in the First Class, seventeen in the Second Class and five in the Third Class.

And I was second from top in the First Class, achieving 78.19%, whilst Master Trott above me only scored slightly higher with 78.57%. After a mere two terms at LCHS I was already making my mark at Geography where I scored 93%, although Master Trott (no doubt a swot or perhaps a more sophisticated creep to Katy Bones, and a lad of whom I have no memory whatsoever) was marked with 95%. I came out top in English with 80% (beating Trott – although he and I both scored B+ for Gym, which in my case beggars belief for I was not what you could call sporty in the least!).

Disaster!

The three top students – First Class to a boy – moved into the A-stream in our second year which, for me, was the worse thing that could have happened.

I was happy coming second and third in class in the B-stream, but up there in the A-stream I was destined for appear around 20th to 23rd out of 25 for the rest of my school life.

My father – who failed to understand the streaming system or, perhaps, just did not want to know – declared that after the glories of my first year, I had become an abject failure in his eyes, having let the family name (in general) and him (in particular) down with an almighty thump that could be heard from Church Road, Newbury Park, to Essex Road, Leyton (although my Mum thought I was a bright lad and a good boy to boot).

Of course, by the same token the five pupils marked Third Class dropped down to the C-stream, including Mead who, I recall, had a mop of bushy unkempt hair. Osborne appears at the bottom of the list with the words *'evacuated during the term'* against his name – I guess his parents decided to send him out of London when the Nazi doodlebugs started to do their worst.

The second photocopy document is the programme for the Distribution of Prizes on Thursday 6th June 1946 at 2.30pm in the School Hall. The guest of honour who would hand out the prizes was none other than Derek McCulloch, OBE, Director, *Children's Hour* at the BBC – Uncle Mac to us all, who brought each afternoon's broadcast on the radio to a much-lamented ending with the immortal words: *"Goodnight children"* followed by a pause - and then *"everywhere!"* to which we all replied: *"Goodnight Uncle Mac"* – well, I did anyway!

My name appears in the list of the eight from the First Year who received Form Prizes – alongside those of the Brilliant and the Talented, including Bradbury (who was just clever but whose mother gave him too much to eat and would have starved herself to do so for food was rationed it being wartime), Morgan (who was also clever, but tall with it, who could run like the wind and was so handsome that girls could barely walk past him without swooning or dropping dead - or both), Pownall (the brighter of the twins for his brother was in the B-stream and was clearly self-conscious of this fact), Venis (who was blond and athletic) and Herring (who was very, very small to the point where he was almost minute – although that may be an exaggeration, but it was over sixty-five years ago).

Enormous

Sadly, so sadly, I was unable to attend this event for I was suffering from the most enormous carbuncle just below the knee on my left leg - which was not only highly painful, but which required a piping hot kaolin poultice to be administered three times a day by my ever-caring and resourceful mother.

I hobbled to see Dr Munroe, whose surgery was on the corner of Brook Road and Aldborough Road South, a few days later. Within a trice the Good Doctor had his scalpel out and the carbuncle was lanced – but decency and a sense of decorum insists that I draw a veil over what gushed out from my bony leg!

Fascinating

We now leap forward five years to Thursday 16th March 1950. I had left school six months earlier, but returned for the Senior School Distribution of Prizes at 7.30pm (the Juniors having had their bash at 2.30pm the same day). That evening I received my General School Certificate alongside thirty-seven of my pals, whilst twenty-six of the more academic tagged Exemption from Matriculation onto their School Cert. What is fascinating is that all the lads who received Form Prizes with me in the First Year Matriculated (including Herring who was so very, very small) – except for me!

But – and here my chest fills with well-deserved pride, even though I say it myself – I am listed under the heading Memorial Prizes – *'awarded for special merit in the subject named and linked with the names of Old Boys who fell in the war of 1914-1918'*. It will come as no surprise to the reader, who has been following this tale closely, to learn that the subject for which I received a Memorial Prize (in memory of J. G. Laurie) was Geography.

And as I walked proudly to the stage, Mrs Cattell-Jones clapped in her black gown, with her mop of grey hair and thick glasses, and I would swear that her false teeth clacked, too.

Bradbury received the Memorial Prize for English, Morgan for Mathematics, Munden for Art and Burr for German. But then they would, wouldn't they! Michael McStay (who Matriculated) received a Subject Prize in English – he is the Michael McStay who went on to star in many a TV drama and a few films – as I have mentioned earlier and will continue to do so whenever it is appropriate, for it is not often that I have brushed shoulders with a TV celebrity.

The address was given by Lt Col A. C. Newman, VC, TD, DL and the prizes were presented by Mrs Newman. Col Newman was a local boy done good. Born in Hertfordshire, he was educated at Bancroft's School – up the road from LCHS and then a Public School - serving in the Territorial Army prior to the Second World War. He was attached to No. 2 Commando, distinguishing himself at the St Nazaire raid on 27th March 1942 for which he received the Victoria Cross.

Later he was Chairman of W & C French who engaged in a mighty lot of house and business building construction in these parts in the post-war era. And that is the chap whose wife handed me my School Cert and the Memorial Prize. Phew!

I was pleased to read that Burgess and Leftkovitch received Memorial Prizes for Music. Both were a year or two ahead of me and in the final two or three years of my time at LCHS they would play at two grand pianos in the school hall – at breaks and lunchtime. At the Distribution of Prizes they played three duets – including Handel's *Entry of the Queen of Sheba* which, in itself, gives some idea of their skill at the pianoforte. They gave such great pleasure to so many of us. I wish I knew what happened to them both.

My thanks to Brian whose photocopies have allowed me to relive this part of my life again.

School dinners

I received an email from Lionel King, now living in the Midlands, who was unable to attend the LCHS 80th Anniversary, but had a report about it from one of his contemporaries, John Sloman.,

Lionel writes: *"You were three or four years my senior - a contemporary of Bradbury, McStay, Kipper Herring, Munden, Gaiteley, Thompson, Stickland, Tolvin, Hart, et alia. You were briefly my table captain at lunch before I was moved on to Johnny Clark's table.*

"You were also in the Geographical Society at the same time. Jane Cattell-Jones adopted me as one of her Geography 'blue-eyed boys' after you left. John Punshon was the other. He went on to take the subject at A Level while I unwisely dropped it after O Level when I had the satisfaction of being top student that year. I studied Languages and was Head Boy in 1954-55. I later graduated from Birmingham University.

"Later I became a Senior Lecturer in Communications in FE. I fought three General Elections for a seat in Parliament 1964-87 but never got anywhere near. So did Punshon on two occasions, 1964-66. He never got there either.

"I do remember you very well as always being smartly dressed. Belsen Bill was rather unkind. Perhaps 'Judge' Jeffries would have been positively cruel! I remember you were very light on your feet. I was always flat-footed. It seems odd writing to someone I have not seen for over 60 years.

"Katie died in the 1980s. I last saw her in the mid 1970s at her home, 'Sunny Lawns', Leytonstone, when she had been retired a few years. She lasted at the School until aged 65 in 1961. I took my daughter Joanna along who was five at that time. Kate was still hale and hearty and still travelling. I couldn't get to her funeral but there was a very good turn-out, I'm told. All the staff are dead now so far as I can gather. They would all be extremely old men if still with us. Cummings died aged 90 in 1999."

He goes on to write about staff and fellow students. I telephoned him later that week. We chatted contentedly for an hour or so. It was all a bit emotional, but I will ring him again.

My recollection of school dinners at LCHS is lost in the mists of time, but my good friend John – who followed me a year of two later at the school and was at the 80th Anniversary – tells me that *"School dinners were treacherous affairs with each table having a 'captain' appointed from the 5th year. The 'fags' as the juniors were called, had to queue at the kitchen hatches, in the corridor behind the stage and between the centre of the rear part of the school and the gym. The trick was to collect tureens of the foul stuff and carry them without accident back to the table whereupon the 'table captain' acted as 'Mum' and dished out the portions to his chums at the table."*

Shoemaker, millwright, carpenter

Yvonne's father died in August 1957. The funeral was held in the village church of St. Andrew, Aldringham, and four weeks later Yvonne and I were back in the same church for our wedding.

Within three weeks Yvonne's mother had moved from their tied cottage on the Ogilvie Estate - where Yvonne's father had been a carpenter - to live in Stowmarket with her parents. And so came to an end an era in Yvonne's life - and mine, too.

It is a remarkable fact that Yvonne's grandfather – her father's father – died fifty-four years before Yvonne was born. Few people can say that about a family relationship; it happened because Yvonne's father was 63 when - following the death of his first wife - he married Yvonne's mother – who was 28.

Grandfather Samuel Friend was born in 1819 and lived all his life in Front Street in the Suffolk village of Wenhaston, where he worked as a shoemaker, until he died in 1879.

He married Sarah Driver, who was twenty-three and seven years younger than him, in June 1849.

They had seven children – Charles (born 1853), Arthur (1859), Ellen (1861), Jane (1864), George (1967), Edward Charles (1870) and Laura (1871, who died in 1898, the same year as her mother).

Yvonne's father, Edward Charles, married his first wife, Clara Jane. We know that Clara Jane was born in the same year as her husband (1870) and that their first daughter, Lillian, was born in 1898, so a shrewd guess would put them as marrying in the late 1890s when they were both in their twenties.

Lillian lived in Peterborough, where she had two daughters, and died in 1976 at the age of seventy-eight.

Edward and Clara's two other daughters died in their teens – Hilda (1899-1917) and Mabel (1902-1916).

Clara – who died in 1931 - and her daughters are all buried in the grounds of what was Aldringham Baptist Chapel.

Yvonne's father – Ted Friend as he was known – worked on the Ogilvie Estate, living in one of four cottages on the Thorpe Road. He was millwright at the Aldringham post mill on the hill behind the Parrot Public

House and as estate carpenter in his workshop next door to his cottage home.

Yvonne's mother, Ethel Maud, was born in 1905. Her father, Henry William Hammond (whose home was in Stowmarket where he worked as a plumber), married Alice Maud Masterson (who was born in Aldringham Post Office, now the Craft Market, opposite the Parrot) on 10th April 1904. Ethel had three siblings – Nellie Ruth (1908-1954), George Masterson (1909-1993) and Jack Christopher Terris (1915-1999).

Ethel was destined for Cambridge University, but was taken ill in her late teens and was unable to fulfil her ambition. Instead, after a long illness during which she lived with her parents, when she was well enough, she went to work as a cook in Aldeburgh and then as live-in housekeeper to Ted Friend after his first wife died in 1931.

Ted and Ethel were married on 25th February 1933 – he was sixty-three and she was twenty-eight – and on 17th December of that year Yvonne was born.

I met Yvonne in the choir stalls at St. Peter's Aldborough Hatch in 1951. We celebrated our Golden Wedding in 2007 – but here I want to recall something about Ted Friend and 'his' windmill (for I will always see it as such).

Ted's windmill

Much of the following is culled from Yvonne's memory and from a leaflet published by a local historical society which we picked up in the mill at Thorpeness during a day visit in 1984.

The Aldringham post mill was built in 1824. An advertisement in the *Suffolk Chronicle* of 1836 describes the mill as *"A capital Post Windmill, erected within the last twelve years, and now in excellent repair, with a Brick Round House, Bins capable of holding ten score of corn and two pairs of French stones . . . well situated at Aldringham, and in full trade; it adjoins the Turnpike Road leading from Leiston and Aldeburgh."*

The 1841 Census lists James Crane as miller and trade directories give the following as millers: 1846, James Crane; 1853, James Fluse; 1858 and 1864, John Walker, who came from Theberton Mill and later moved to a mill at Aldeburgh. The 1871 Census gives Robert Rackham as miller, and although resident in the parish in 1861, he had "aged" from twenty-four to thirty-eight in the intervening ten years! By 1875 Francis Skoulding was the miller and in 1892 Samuel King.

In the 1890s the mill was included in land purchased by the Ogilvie family, and became part of the Sizewell Estate. At this time John Oxborrow was grinding grist for cattle food, and he continued milling up to 1921 when the mill was moved to Thorpeness.

Since 1910 the estate owner, Glencairn Stuart Ogilvie, had been creating a

(Above) The post mill at Thorpeness built in 1824 - photographed in 2006 during a family visit to Yvonne's home village.

'model' seaside village at what had previously been the fishing hamlet of Thorpe. By the early 192Os, the Meare (an inland lake) had been created, the Country Club opened and about forty houses of distinctive design built. The aim was to deliberately create a small holiday village. The whole project was carefully planned, including the provision of services such as water and electricity. Water of exceptional purity was obtained from a well twenty-eight feet deep on the site of the present mill. It was at first pumped up by an annular-sailed iron wind pump with a large storage tank on the top.

After the First World War it was decided to replace the iron wind pump with a mill more fitting to the attractive resort. As the Aldringham post mill was on the estate and nearby, this was chosen.

The removal was completed in the winter of 1922-23. Ted Friend, the estate carpenter (and Yvonne's father, whose photograph appears in my autobiography *Just an Essex Lad*) supervised the removal, while Amos Clarke and his son, local millwrights, were engaged to do the dismantling and re-erection. They had intended to convey the complete body of the mill on a timber wagon but the whole mill had to be dismantled piece by piece for fear of damaging the unmade roads.

During the 1939-1945 war children blocked the fantail rack and a gale pushed the mill off its post, leaving the fan carriage in mid-air. Mickey Staff, the estate foreman, used fifty servicemen in a vain attempt to correct the tilt, but in the end millwright Ted Friend was called in and after climbing over the inside of the mill, gave a few blows with his hammer which settled the mill back to its correct position.

"They know me round here"

I have fond memories of Ted Friend during the six years that I knew him. A gentle man of great wisdom and patience, he had difficulty in coming to terms with the changes that were taking place around him – for he was eighty-one when I first met him. He would walk slowly in the middle of the road, eschewing the concern of family and friends that he might be hit by a passing car with the wry comment: *"But they all know me round here!"*

Ted never travelled far from his home County – visiting London once or twice when he was younger and Ipswich a few more times – but never abroad.

When Yvonne was a girl at home – up until 1950 - water was pumped from a well behind the cottage, they had gas but no electricity, baths were taken in a tin tub in front of the fire with the water being heated in a copper in the wash-house across the yard, and sanitation involved digging holes in the fields behind the cottages to bury – but I will not go into details.

Ted loved his garden in front of the cottage and his allotment a few steps away up the road towards the sea, where he grew sufficient vegetables to feed his family throughout the year.

I am glad I knew him – albeit it briefly.

The boatyard in the churchyard

I was contacted in September 2009 by Roderic Findlay, the son of Doctor Findlay, whose GP practice was at Number One Spearpoint Gardens, just down the road from where I live, in the 1950s.

Dr Findlay moved from Aldborough Hatch on his appointment as Regional Medical Officer for Lincolnshire in the late 1950s and died in 1976. His widow – 96 in 2009 and in good health – has her home near Bridport.

(Above) A somewhat faded press clipping from the 'Ilford Recorder' showing the 'Eagle' being lowered into the River Roding at Ilford Broadway.

Roderic, recently retired from teaching history, lives in Bridport, Dorset, where he runs a small printing business. Roderic was a Sea Scout in the 1st Aldborough Hatch (St. Peter's) Scout Group and was helpful in enabling me to write this story for publication in the St. Peter's BROADSHEET in January 2010 – adding his memories to mine.

Few residents of today's Aldborough Hatch will know that there was once a thriving group of Sea Scouts based at St. Peter's, nor would they be aware that the dozen or so youngsters in their blue jerseys and sailor's hats built a sailing dinghy on the edge of the churchyard.

57

The 1st Aldborough Hatch (St. Peter's) Scout Group had started before the Second World War in the 1930s, reopening after the War in 1946. In the early 1950s, Derek Williams, who taught woodwork at a local secondary school, was one of the team of young leaders in the Group. Keen on boating and the sea, Derek persuaded the Group to let him lead a Patrol of Sea Scouts within the Scout Troop – named the Eagle Patrol. Soon Derek realised that building a dinghy of their own would mean that the Sea Scouts could enjoy sailing all year round.

At that time the church halls at St. Peter's remained much as when they were built in 1867 – the large hall fronting Aldborough Road North and the Vestry Room at the North West corner were erected much later - in the late 1950s.

The open ground where the Vestry Room now stands became a boatyard where the Sea Scouts spent several hot summers and bitterly cold winters building an 18 foot National Dinghy under the shelter of a canvas covering to keep off the worst of the weather.

It would have been a considerable achievement for experienced boat builders working in the crude workshop, but what was even more remarkable was the fact that Derek – an experienced woodworker – insisted that the Sea Scouts did every bit of the boat building themselves under his expert tuition, right down to steaming the planks to make the shape of the keel.

Conveyed on a low loader from St. Peter's to the River Roding below Ilford Hill where the dinghy entered the water, the Sea Scouts rowed downstream to the River Thames.

With sails hoisted, the *Eagle* – for that was how she was named - moved majestically up river towards London's world-famous Tower Bridge, which was to be opened specially so that the TV cameras from the *BBC's Blue Peter* could film this momentous occasion (the opening of the bridge was to add excitement to the event for the *Eagle* could have sailed below the road bridge with plenty of headroom to spare!).

Roderic recalls that a hitch in hoisting the mainsail just as the dinghy approached Tower Bridge meant that the *Eagle* went through stern first with the tide. But no matter – for the Sea Scouts in particular and Aldborough Hatch in general made TV history.

"We had some wonderful times sailing the 'Eagle'," Roderic remembers, *"going down to Leigh-on-Sea by train and sailing right across the Thames estuary.*

"I was sent away to boarding school and later the Sea Scouts split off and became 4th Seven Kings. They met in Downshall Junior School, which was closed in the school holidays, so there were no meetings when I was at home and I lost touch. But it was never the same after it split off and a number of the Sea Scouts returned to the 1st Aldborough Hatch, including Den Day, Geoff Griffiths and Colin Woodcock. Other names I remember

The Vicar of Aldborough Hatch at the time of the launch of the 'Eagle' was the Rev Lawrence Pickles, seen (above) canoeing on the lake in the Vicarage Garden. His widowed mother stands on the bank. The Vicarage was demolished when the garden and meadow were sold to a builder in the 1960s by the then Vicar. Today's Vicarage and the homes in St. Peter's Close were built, but sadly the garden and meadow – where camping and outdoor activities were enjoyed by youngsters - were lost for ever to the local community.

from the Sea Scouts were Brian Greenhow, Terry Woods, our Patrol Leader, Nobby Clark from Bawdsey Avenue, Geoff Coles, Alan Belcher who went out with Christine from the flats near us at Aldborough Court and was good at things electrical, and Kenneth Chapman from Roy Gardens."

Ecumenical

Roderic had what might be described as an ecumenical upbringing as a boy in Aldborough Hatch. *"I went to the Sunday School at Oaks Lane Methodist Church with my friend, Graham Tulloch who lived at 5 Ramsgill Drive - and a very good Sunday School it was – but I was baptised by Mr. Byng when I was seven and confirmed by the Bishop of Barking when I was twelve and loved the services at St. Peter's in Lawrence Pickles' time.*

"I went with my mother to take tea at the Vicarage with Favil Greer, the daughter of the Rev Joseph Palanque Byng and Mrs Byng. I am glad Twopence, Favil and David's son, is remembered in the recently published booklet 'From Westminster to Aldborough Hatch – A History of St. Peter's Church'. He was a dear little boy and it was very sad when he was drowned so tragically in the Vicarage lake in 1949. I remember that Favil

organised a party of children to go Bertram Mill's Circus at London's Olympia in the late 1940s and I went with them.

"There were a lot of very good people living in Aldborough Hatch at that time. I remember especially the Thompsons, who owned the newsagents next door to my father's surgery, Mr and Mrs Middleton at the chemists on Silverdale Parade, and Mr and Mrs Perry, the butchers, who came to evensong every week."

Plank-steaming in the churchyard

Following publication in the BROADSHEET of the story about the building of the *Eagle* in the churchyard at St. Peter's, I received an email from Alan and Christine Belcher, both of whom were mentioned in the article.

Married for 49 years and now living in Suffolk, Alan and Christine had been leaders in Scout Groups after moving from Aldborough Hatch following their marriage.

They told us that the article *"evoked such wonderful memories of that period in our lives"*. In their message, Alan recalled the building of the *Eagle* on the ground where the Vestry Room now stands in St. Peter's Churchyard.

Tragically, Alan died in February 2010 shortly after writing, having been bedridden for some months with Myloid Leukaemia. Alan wrote:

"My experience in the Scouts and the Sea Scouts had a profound effect on my life and I have always been very grateful for the wood-working skills and the experience I gained during the building of the Eagle.

"I remember particularly the plank steaming weekends when we had to saw the 20 foot left and right hand planks, shaping each one individually and spending hours planing and sanding them in order to achieve Scout Leader Derek William's exacting standards. These then required steaming in order that they could be bent to shape and fixed to the oak frame.

"We never seemed to have enough coal for heating the large water drum required for the steaming process, so in the build-up to the steam weekends we had the task of convincing parents and neighbours that they needed bundles of our scrap wood, which we had gathered together, for their fires. In exchange for this they would give us the necessary coal.

"In this way we always managed a good roaring fire, as all good Scouts would. I can remember the acrid smell of the smoke drifting across the adjoining graveyard as we stoked the fire in our efforts to keep up the head of steam required to complete the work. Our actions caused many complaints from people tending graves!

"The next stage was for Derek to give the OK for the scalding hot planks to be removed and for us young Scouts to run around trying to clamp the planks into position before they lost their elasticity - something, I'm sure, that would never be allowed today for health and safety reasons. All this was completed under the watchful eye of Derek."

They said it was impossible

Shortly after the launch of the *Eagle,* Derek and his Sea Scouts formed their own Scout Group – the 4th Seven Kings - moving away from St. Peter's to meet at Downshall School, a mile or so down Aldborough Road. A decade of so later I was present at the launch of the *Seven Kings,* a 44 foot, six-and-a-half- ton yacht, on the Essex Coast.

Built by the Sea Scouts under Derek's direction at Hargreaves Scout Camp Site in Hainault Road, less than a mile away from St. Peter's, it was a massive undertaking, which received national coverage.

I wrote the following at that time for The Scout Association's publication *SCOUTING 70* which I edited.

"Early one sunny morning in April, 1969, a boy-built yacht slipped smoothly into the waters of an Essex estuary. A wind-whipped spray and biting cold could not dampen the enthusiasm of the five hundred people who had travelled to this bleak shore to see the fulfilment of a dream - a dream that had confounded the experts.

"Seven years ago they said that the task of building a yacht of this size was impossible! In itself there is nothing remarkable in the building of a yacht. Similar boats are launched around the coasts of Britain every year. What is remarkable - and what makes the story worth telling - is the fact that the *Seven Kings* was built on the outskirts of London by enthusiastic young members of a Sea Scout Group – and it was that which they said was impossible. Derek Williams, Group Scout Leader of the 4th Seven Kings Scout Group, masterminded the project from the beginning.

"Seven years ago it was decided that the ownership of a vessel was the only satisfactory way to provide for the boys of the Group training which the responsibility of crewing a yacht gives. To buy a yacht was out of the question. So the Group decided to build one for themselves.

"They knew from the beginning that this was the largest boat-building project ever tackled by any youth organisation and were determined to build to Lloyd's 100 A1 + classification standards.

"Ilford East District Scout Council set aside a corner of their District Camp Site and Training Centre at Hargreaves on the edge of London's Green Belt. For seven years the building of the boat attracted visitors from many parts of this country and abroad.

"More than 25,000 boy and man hours were poured into the project. Now the Group owns a magnificent craft valued at over £18,000. It required infinite patience and skill as well as brawn.

"Seven-and-a-half years is a long time - especially for the young. But a mark of the Scouts' enthusiasm and belief in the worth of the project is the fact that many of the 12-year-olds who helped to cut out the keel have grown up with the yacht and are still keenly associated with it."

61

Of Sugar Sunday, Pickling Sunday, Raffles and the like

Until the first half of the 19th Century, Hainault Forest in Essex came down to Aldborough Hatch and the word 'Hatch' itself denoted a hatch or gate into the forestland. In 1851, an Act of Parliament 'disafforested' Hainault and 100,000 trees on Crown land were felled within two years.

Large farms were laid out on Fairlop Plain with housing for labourers and the straight roads - Hainault Road, Forest Road and New North Road - were cut through.

Aldborough Hatch, once described as "the village in the suburbs", stretches from the South of Fairlop Plain and, not unnaturally, a number of myths and legends have grown up over the years.

Amongst these are two special Sundays – Sugar Sunday and Pickling Sunday – neither of which are known or celebrated (as far as we are aware) outside the Hatch (in general) and St. Peter's Church (in particular).

It has been said that their origins lie in the *Book of Common Prayer*, but I regret to say that despite intensive research (which, at times, was quite painful), I have been unable to verify the accuracy of that statement.

The first prayer book was published in 1549 in the reign of Edward VI, following the break with Rome and a bit before my time. This was rapidly succeeded by a reformed revision in 1552, under the same editorial hand, that of Thomas Cranmer, Archbishop of Canterbury, and a combined version appeared in 1559. Tumultuous events over the next century, including the English Civil War (of which I have no personal experience), meant that it was not until 1662 that what became the official prayer book of the Church of England – also called the *Book of Common Prayer* – hit the bookshops.

Things stayed very much the same until the last century when an edition was published *"with the additions and deviations proposed in 1928"*, followed by the *Alternative Service Book 1980*, and later *Common Worship.* I have searched them all – well, most of them anyway – and both Sundays are conspicuous by their absence.

Sugar Sunday takes place at St. Peter's by decree of the Parochial Church Council, usually in September, when members of the congregation will stagger from their cars, motor cycles and bicycles, or hobble up the road – often leaning heavily on walking sticks and zimmer frames - laden down with bags and bags (and in some cases sacks) of granulated, icing or castor sugar to be laid in the pews at the back of the church.

My research (for I am nothing if not thorough) reveals that there are some sixty different sugars known to man – including Beet sugar, Grape sugar, Gur, Invert, Jaggery, Rock, Sanding and Superfine.

(Above) St. Peter's Church today – scene of the unique Sugar Sunday and Pickling Sunday – and where no social or fund-raising event is complete without a raffle.

But the ladies of Peter's ask for none of these – just the three named – although I would guess that a few bags of Superfine would be welcomed, but unlikely, for this is manufactured in the USA.

And why, I hear you cry, is all this sugar required – and in such vast quantities? Let me explain – if you are still with me, that is. The major event in the Aldborough Hatch winter social calendar is the St. Peter's Christmas Bazaar. For this the ladies of the parish stir huge cauldrons of jams (using home-grown fruits, such as plums, damsons and cherry plums – the latter growing in abundance in the Shrubberies, a mere stone's throw from where I live) and marmalades (where the fruit is imported, for oranges do not do well hereabouts).

And before some clever dick tells me that the Seville Orange season is not in the autumn, I would point out that some of the sugar will be stored until the following year when the stalls in Romford Market groan under the weight of that succulent fruit. Meantime, a tinned marmalade preparation will be used by those who missed the Seville season (and there are not many who do so, for these ladies are canny to say the least, and they prefer the fresh fruits to those in tins).

And the types of marmalade will be many and various – lemon marmalade and whiskey marmalade being amongst the most popular.

(Above) Home-made jams, marmalades and pickled onions on the stall at the St. Peter's Christmas Bazaar, served by some of the jam-makers and picklers.

Whiskey marmalade is especially popular with those who like to start the day with a bang and not a whimper.

Sugar is also a vital ingredient of the many different varieties of cake that will adorn the stall of that name at the Christmas Bazaar and the ladies who slave over hot stoves for days on end will welcome the sugar supplies as they come tumbling in. And Jean, who stocks a superb stall at the St. Peter's Flower Festival with her delicious array of home-made sweets, will store some of the sugar in a dry place to be used in the days running up to that Festival the following June.

Pickling and Picklers

And so to Pickling Sunday which takes place in October, on the first Sunday in the half term week, an important factor when fixing this date, as I will explain later. A few days prior to the Sunday, sacks of pickling onions are purchased by the Most Senior Picklers and conveyed to the Church Halls.

At around 2.30pm on Pickling Sunday (having partaken of the customary roast beef, Yorkshire puddings, roast potatoes, sprouts and all the trimmings, followed by liberal helpings of plum duff and custard), a motley crew of Picklers descends upon the Church Halls. They are hiding their cutting boards and pickling knives under their skirts and up their shirts lest they be accused by the local constabulary of carrying an offensive weapon or going equipped for theft - for some (but not all) of them have what might be described as a furtive manner as they slink along Aldborough Road North.

Large tables are arranged in a square in the centre of the hall with a number of bowls – some filled with onions in their prime state and wallowing around in clean water, others waiting to receive peeled onions and yet more to collect the discarded skins.

The Senior (and self-appointed) Pickler invites any who may be new to the task to watch as she deftly despatches the brown, crinkly skin of an onion into one bowl and the fresh white onion into another. Various methods of removing the skin are offered to the novice.

Personally I prefer the 'top' and 'tail' method, whereby the onion is held firmly on the cutting board and its 'top' and 'tail' are removed with a swift cut with the knife – for the remaining skin tends to fall away without complaint.

Depending on which Picklers turn up to take part, the conversation around the pickling tables will be either enthralling or as dull at ditch water as tales of previous pickling sessions are exchanged, interlaced with the latest parish gossip – of which there can be much.

(Above) The new season's pickled onions on sale on the preserves stall at the St. Peter's Christmas Bazaar in good time for the festive season.

The Big Moment will be awaited in eager anticipation - for no-one has mentioned, prior to Pickling Sunday or on the day itself, that there will be self-induced tearfulness, something that experienced Picklers look forward to in the days, weeks and months leading up to the Big Day. Almost invariably the first person to cry will be a novice as the experienced Picklers roll about in uncontrollable laughter. However, the air soon fills with onion vapour and before you could shout *"Call the Archdeacon!"* or *"Not 'Guide me, O though great Redeemer' again, Vicar!"* more and more of the Picklers are shedding tears. Tables and floor fast become awash with both water from the peeling and from the tears – but relief is at hand, as the last few onions are lifted from the sacks.

It should be mentioned that the onion skins so deftly removed are not discarded to landfill, but carried in a black plastic sack to the home of Ruth, whose ancient tortoise hibernates over the winter months in the compost heap at the bottom of Ruth's garden – snug in a bed of onion skins.

The Picklers retire to their homes, sure in the knowledge that come Boxing Day when the cold turkey and ham are on the festive table, the centrepiece of the buffet will be St. Peter's Pickled Onions – fresh, gleaming, crunchy and sharp to the taste.

What happens after the Picklers depart and until the jars of St. Peter's Pickled Onions appear on the preserves stall at the Christmas Bazaar is a dark and closely guarded secret known only to the most Senior and Revered Chief Picklers. Their lips remain sealed from year to year, but occasionally titbits will leak out. For example, the half-term week is chosen to allow the pickling process to take place in the Church Hall kitchen, undisturbed by the tiny feet of the Pre-School Day Nursery, whose members will also be on their holidays. Salt and vinegar are involved, but the why and the what are not divulged.

"When two or three are gathered together"

Finally there are the St. Peter's Raffles. In days of yore, when cash was needed to repair the drains, replace the tiles on the roof or extend the churchyard, the favourite fund-raiser at St. Peter's was the whist drive.

In the 1940s Mrs Cooper, wife of the Churchwarden named (not surprisingly) Mr Cooper, would call upon all and sundry to attend a *"little Whist Drive"*.

I heard recently from an acquaintance of the Coopers that when they retired and moved to the South Coast, Mrs Cooper continued to exhort both friends and enemies to attend one of her *"little Whist drives"*.

Nowadays, whist drives have disappeared from the scene and the raffle is the flavour of the month – and has been for some years.

I have heard it said on more than one occasion that *"when two or three are gathered together at St. Peter's, there shall be a raffle"*. Indeed I have been told that this injunction appears in the 1662 *Book of Common Prayer,* but whilst I cannot claim to have read every word and every page, I have to say that – yet again - I have not been able to verify this statement. If you find it, please let me know – a note on the back of a fiver posted through my door would do fine.

In most cases the prizes for the raffles are the sort of things you would be happy to win, but at other times this is not the case. There have been raffles when I have prayed that my number will not be pulled out and I have even been known not to place the second part of my raffle ticket in the basket from which the winners are to be drawn. Bottles of wine give the impression that they might be worth winning, but it is a fact that some of the bottles that appear have been doing the rounds of the St. Peter's raffles since I was a boy – if not before!

If another of your tickets is drawn after you have received a prize, it is considered bad form to take another goody. One is expected to do the decent thing and ask for the ticket to be redrawn.

From time to time there will be a cad amongst us who does not observe this unwritten rule. We are all too polite to say anything, but if looks could kill, the perpetrator of this dastardly crime would be a goner within seconds.

Bread for prisoners

Publication of my autobiography, *Just an Essex Lad,* had one unexpected spin-off for me – I found myself in touch again with friends from the past and with folk I had never met. For many reading my book brought memories flooding back of Aldborough Hatch before, during and after the 1939-45 War. One of these was Bernard Thomas, who was a Queen's Scout in the 1st Aldborough Hatch (St. Peter's) Scout Group. He represented Ilford East at the World Scout Jamboree at Niagara on the Lake in 1955 and worked with me in the 1950s as an Assistant Cub Scout Leader in the 1st Aldborough Hatch. Bernard's recollections appeared in the November 2009 St. Peter's BROADSHEET – as follows:

"I was born in the Children's Hospital in Hackney, moving to Leyswood Drive when I was nine-months-old in 1939. We must have been 'posh' according to Ron's book because our house was semi-detached with a garage. I remember the sweet shop and café on the hill at Newbury Park Station, the coal office, the Co-op at the Green Gate, Nan's Pantry, Sainsbury's at Gants Hill, and the wet fish shop and Middleton's the chemist on Silverdale Parade.

"Cutmore was the baker's shop on Silverdale Parade. We bought loaves of bread for the Italian prisoners of war – who were always hungry - when they were building the Oaks Lane estate which was just past where

Homefield Avenue headed West. Previously there were only fields between Leyswood Drive, Roy Gardens and Oaks Lane.

"My cousin Brian, who lived at Forest Gate, married the Chemist's daughter Joyce Middleton. Sadly Brian died, but Joyce lives in Hutton and is in touch with William Torbitt School friends. I remember Mr. Train, Head Teacher at the Torbitt, and teachers Miss Billington and Miss Ball.

"My Dad kept rabbits (Flemish Giants and Dutch Angoras), chickens (Black and White Leghorns, Buff Rocks and Rhode Island Reds) and also some ducks (Khaki Campbell). I used to spray them with a hose-pipe and they would stand up and ask for more.

"I cycled weekly to Biggs in Brook Road to buy fish meal, bone meal, shell grit, limestone and 'Karswood', a red powder for making the yolks bright yellow - tasks I had to perform to earn my threepence a week pocket money. I was probably about eight or nine at the time. I collected dandelion leaves for the rabbits and I remember the awful smell of the chicken hash that Mum used to cook on the stove. We regularly ate rabbit or chicken, and I hated it when Dad killed our pet ones. Eric, my elder brother, refused to eat his. Dad had to buy it off him and Mum had to cook him scrambled egg.

"We also collected shrapnel which we took to an ARP post at the entrance to the sports' ground in Oaks Lane, just past Crownfield Avenue (where Oaks Park High School stands today). We were paid if we had a bucketful. Our milk was delivered by horse and cart and if the horse did 'their jobs', I was sent post haste with a bucket to collect it. Apparently it was good for the rhubarb.

"At the beginning of the War, we were evacuated to Devon, but Mum cried all the way there and Dad fetched her home the following week after which we lived in Leyswood Drive through all the bombing raids.

"We had our roof removed by the bomb which exploded in the William Torbitt School playing fields – the blast came through the gap in the houses opposite that back onto the fields, blowing the front door through the house and the kitchen door into the garden at the rear. I think we had three weeks off whilst they repaired all the windows."

From East Prussia to Aldborough Hatch

Pauline Iles (now living in Hertfordshire) contacted me, recalling that her father – who had been a German prisoner of war – worked on Aldborough Hall Farm. Here is her story:

"Paul Zuch was born on 14th July 1922 in the village of Krämersdorf, near Allenstein in East Prussia, which is now Kromerowo, near Olsztyn in Poland. In March 1940, aged 17, he joined the Luftwaffe becoming a pilot, first flying Fieseler Storch aeroplanes and then being transferred to Communications. He served with the Luftwaffe in Scandinavia, Russia, Italy and finally France where, shortly after D-day, he and the remnants of his regiment surrendered to the Americans just outside Rouen.

"In September 1944 he was taken from Cherbourg to Southampton on the *Queen Mary.* The next stop was Liverpool and from there on a Canadian ship to New York. After 18 months at different PoW camps he was finally told in January 1946 that he was going home and was put on a ship bound for Germany, but it docked at Liverpool because of an engine problem."

This photograph of farm workers on Aldborough Hall Farm was taken in the early 1950s showing (from the left) Len Patient, Ron Seward. Paul Zuch and (with the spade) George Gansbühler. Len and Edna Patient had two sons, Alan and David. They moved to Abridge and retired in Loughton. Ron and Edith Seward lived in Painters Road with their son, John. They moved to Wall Hall College, Aldenham near Watford, where Ron worked with Paul Zuch as a gardener. Ron and John died, but Edith lived in her 90s in a residential home in Wiltshire when Pauline wrote to me in 2009. George and Pat Gansbühler and their sons, George, Robert and Richard, moved to East Ham where they ran a corner shop. George had been a German PoW. They retired to Northampton.

"There they were taken off and a series of more camps followed – Manchester, Raynes Park, Dingwall in Scotland and High Garrett, Essex, by which time he had been demobbed. He knew that his homeland of East Prussia was gone and was now under Polish Communist control so he applied for and was granted permission to stay in England.

"During this time he had met Florence and they married in 1948 in Hackney before moving to Aldborough Hall Farm where I was born in 1951. I was baptised by the Rev Lawrence Pickles in St. Peter's, where my Godparents were listed as John Chilver, Desmond Mills and Gladys Young – although I do not know anything about them.

"Sadly Florence died in 1954 at the age of 26 and is buried in St Peter's churchyard.

"Paul married again in 1955. Two more children were born and the family moved from Aldborough Hall Farm to Watford in 1957. After retiring as head gardener at Wall Hall College, my father moved to Exeter where he died in 2004. His second wife died in 2005."

The night Grace died

Thursday 22nd September 1955 stands out in my memory for it was the night that Grace Archer died in her husband's arms whilst trying to rescue her horse from a fire in its stable in the village of Ambridge.

I was living at my mother's home at the time when just after seven that evening, the neighbours stood at their front doors, many weeping as they called to friends to share in their grief. And not only was this scene of immediate mourning played out in Church Road, Newbury Park, Ilford, Essex, but up and down the land and throughout the nation.

What few of us appreciated at the time was that this was a piece of competitive scheduling by the BBC – for it was the night on which commercial television was launched.

Twenty million listeners tuned into the long-running radio soap *The Archers* that night and the BBC switchboard was jammed for 48 hours.

I was reminded of this in October 2009 when Norman Painting, the actor who played Phil Archer, husband of the said Grace, in *The Archers,* died aged 85 and his obituary in *The Guardian* brought the memory back.

Whilst Phil (the character) and Norman (the actor) were a few years older than me, there was an affinity between us as our careers in voluntary work followed a similar pattern. Phil was one-time Scout Leader of the Ambridge Scout Group and was later sworn in as a justice of the peace – two roles that I filled hereabouts at around the same time.

I learned from the obituary that Edward Mason and Geoffrey Webb, the *Dick Barton* scriptwriters, worked on *The Archers* scripts for the first twenty years. I recall the sense of sadness and loss that overcame me when Dick Barton and his sidekick Snowy disappeared from the air waves to be replaced by an everyday story of country folk – *The Archers.*

I was bereft for it was as though my right arm had been snapped off (and I can sing the Dick Barton theme tune even now if you wish me to do so – and even if you would prefer not).

But it did mean that Johnny Dearlove arrived on time at Wolf Cub Meetings on Monday evenings. Johnny would run from his bungalow home on the corner of Oaks Lane opposite the Vicarage into the church hall at St. Peter's as the strains of the *Dick Barton, Special Agent,* signature tune died away to be admonished by Mr T, then Group Scout Leader, for arriving late. Johnny would not be put out, pointing out in his best BBC English voice (for his mother was a big noise in the St. Peter's Mothers' Union) to Mr T that *Dick Barton* was educational – which was more than could be said for the first ten minutes of the Cub Meeting when inspection took place and finger nails and polished shoes were examined in close detail.

Johnny, incidentally, went on to lecture as a professor at the University of Sussex – and I guess that *Dick Barton* and the Cubs played a part in that.

The death of the three-legged dog

The untimely death of Tramp, the three-legged dog, occurred on Boxing Day many, many years ago. Tramp was one of a succession of dogs owned and much-loved by Auntie Una, Mrs Una Paul, who lived up the road at Number 55 Spearpoint Gardens, here in Aldborough Hatch. Everyone called her Auntie Una from the day when Heather, our daughter, did so on learning that Auntie Una was her Godmother.

Tramp disappeared one day and was away for some three months or so. Auntie Una was distraught and did everything within her power to find him and bring him back to where he rightly belonged.

Auntie Una and Tramp were well-known in these parts, often to be seen taking early morning and late evening walks, always followed by Pusskins, the Cat, who seemed to enjoy these walkies, strolling at a respectful distance, sometimes running from one front garden to the next, occasionally galloping along the tops of garden walls and infrequently walking on the pavement. All three were much-loved in the Hatch and Tramp was sorely missed.

I cannot recall how Auntie Una found out that Tramp was at Stratford Railway Station. He had been spotted beside the railway line running off to Liverpool Street – with one leg missing. The Vet did what he could and Tramp found that he could manage just as well on three legs as four. Soon the walks resumed and all was well in the Hatch – until Boxing Day that is.

Auntie Una, Granddaughter Helen and the three-legged Tramp spent Christmas with us. Indeed, Auntie Una spent every Christmas with us, for it was not Christmas until Auntie Una arrived at our house on Christmas Eve clutching a couple of sherry trifles – one of which would have more than a little sherry and a few other things beside.

Auntie Una was partial to a glass or three of whiskey – the bottle I bought each year was an investment for it meant that Una would snooze, leaving me to read my Christmas books.

But after lunch on this particular Boxing Day the three-legged Tramp collapsed in front of our sideboard in the dining room and had to be carried home and nursed by Helen. Later that day, sadly, Tramp died in Auntie Una's arms.

"Bring a spade . . . "

It was at this point where I was called upon to assist. *"Bring a spade,"* called Auntie Una down the telephone, *"and wear a strong pair of boots for you will be digging Tramp's grave under the apple tree."*

And when Auntie Una told you to put your boots on and bring a spade, you did just that – and quickly. No messing.

Now it is a fact of which I was unaware at this point that the roots of apple trees are numerous and meander about in the soil below the surface in contortions the like of which you would never believe. Dig I did – but every so often I would reach a root that was immovable.

It was at this point when Auntie Una decided that some professional advice was needed and Farmer Rudge was summoned to appear from up the road in Auntie Una's garden, there to supervise the digging – by me!

I should perhaps mention that the death occurred after lunch when I had enjoyed cold turkey and all the trimmings with a glass or two of wine to wash it all down. I was, to put it bluntly, slightly inebriated and unable to focus clearly all the time.

This did not help with digging as will be appreciated and Auntie Una was not best pleased as I stumbled about, bleary eyed, grumbling about the roots of apple trees. The rest of that afternoon is something of a blur.

Annoyed

On 14th November 2009 storm clouds had hung about since daybreak, as squally winds alternated with heavy downpours of rain – the sort of day when it is comforting to be indoors in the warm with the promise of a good book for the evening.

Sitting at my desk in the office in the afternoon I was joined by Yvonne who had decided to sort through a drawer of papers in her bureau - on the pretext that she needed more space.

Yvonne had discovered a stack of papers from the past, mainly youngest son Richard's school reports, certificates from the Cubs and Scouts, College and elsewhere. Amongst them is an exercise book when Richard was at St Edward's Church of England School in Form 2.4 with Miss Smith. On one page he writes in answer to the statement: *These really annoy me about other people:*

(1) People taking the mickey out of black people;
(2) People never washing;
(3) Vegetarians;
(4) Punks.

Fascinating! I guess he still is annoyed by the above, except (3) for he is now one himself! We will not embarrass Richard with further revelations. but should he misbehave, we will have these on standby.

Where is Kate Adie?

I have long believed that the secret to having a letter published in a national daily newspaper is brevity. In my time I have had two or possibly three letters in *The Guardian,* including one on 26th September 2001 when the invasion of Iraq loomed which read:

"Where is Kate Adie? We need to know. How else can we be sure where it's all happening?"

At that time Kate Adie was a senior war correspondent at the BBC and had disappeared from our TV screens.

My email address was quoted at the end of the letter. My good friend Lee sent me a message to advise me that he had seen her entering Sainsbury's in Barkingside.

Why am I reminded of this? At Yvonne's instigation I have commenced the task of sorting out papers in the office and came across the cutting. Who knows what else I will unearth?

The mystery of the Jewish grave at St. Peter's

From time to time a group gathers to pray at a particular grave in St. Peter's churchyard here in Aldborough Hatch.

On leaving they follow the Jewish tradition of placing a pebble or stone on top of the gravestone to signify that someone has honoured the deceased person's memory with a visit to the grave.

Those of us who have been privileged to witness the gathering have been struck by the dignity of the participants and the solemnity of the occasion.

The grave, which may be found on the lefthandside inside the main gate from Aldborough Road North, has an interesting history linking St. Peter's with the airfields on the open land to the North of the church.

There are said to have been three airfields on Fairlop Plain in the First World War (1914-1918) – Hainault Farm Aerodrome (on land to the East of Hainault Road) and Fairlop Aerodrome – both Royal Naval Air Service - and one of the first Royal Flying Corps airfields which started to operate there from 1915.

Twelve service personnel died on active duty from Hainault Farm Aerodrome and the same number from Fairlop Aerodrome.

Sopwith Camels, single-seat biplane fighters, were based at the farms and the pilots were involved in shooting down Zeppelins. The 44th Squadron Royal Flying Corps was formed at Hainault Farm on 24th July 1917 as a home defence squadron, gaining fame by pioneering the use of the Sopwith Camel for night operations and achieving the first unqualified victory in combat between aircraft flying at night - two Sopwith Camels versus a German Gotha on the night of 28th/29th January 1918.

The buildings standing today on the East side of Hainault Road, opposite Hainault Farm, are Hangers dating back to the First World War.

73

(Above) The grave of Second Lieutenant Jassby in the churchyard at St. Peter's

They were almost certainly used in the Second World War (1939-1945) as no permanent Hangers for maintenance were built on Fairlop Airfield.

Fairlop Airfield was built in 1939 as an auxiliary airfield to cover Hornchurch, Debden and North Weald in the event of them being unusable through enemy attack.

During the Second World War over 1,000 personnel were stationed on Fairlop Plain. Spitfires, Mustangs and Typhoons were amongst the aircraft which flew from Fairlop.

Many service men and women were killed in action and lie buried in Barkingside Cemetery, in the churchyard at Holy Trinity Parish Church, Barkingside, and at St. Mary's Great Ilford. Others killed in action after they flew from Fairlop now lie at peace in various cemeteries in Europe and a few have no known grave.

One serviceman from the First World War lies buried at St. Peter's - in the grave inside the front gate which is visited regularly by members of the local Jewish community. It is the grave of Second Lieutenant Harry Walter Jassby, who was from Montreal, Quebec, Canada. He joined the Royal Flying Corps (forerunner of the Royal Air Force) in 1917 and arrived in England in April 1918. He died in a flying accident seven months later on

74

6th November 1918, just five days before the Armistice was signed on 11th November.

He lied about his age when he enlisted and his gravestone indicates that he was 22, when in fact he was just 20. Before going overseas, he learned to fly during his training as an aerial gunner and was made a Second Lieutenant.

It is highly probable - although we cannot be certain - that Second Lieutenant Jassby was a member of the 44th Squadron Royal Flying Corps as the Squadron remained at Hainault Farm until 1919 when it was disbanded.

The Star of David together with the insignia of the Royal Air Force appears on his tombstone with the inscription:

> In life he flew the azure sky,
> in death he flew to heaven high.

He received a Jewish burial service with military honours. Nothing more is known of Second Lieutenant Jassby or of his family, and why he was buried in the churchyard of St. Peter's remains a mystery.

To hear again the message of the angels

Sitting in the back row of pews at St. Peter's, I waited as choir and congregation prepared to *"to hear again the message of the angels, and in heart and mind to go even unto Bethlehem and see this thing which is come to pass"* at the Service of Nine Lessons and Carols.

In the recent past this service has been held on the Fourth Sunday of Advent, but in 2009 the choirs of St. John, Seven Kings, and St. Peter combined – with the carol service here at St. Peter's on the Third Sunday of Advent and repeated at St. John's on the Fourth.

An innovation in 2009 found all members of the congregation handed a white candle with cardboard collar as they entered the church. These were lit for the singing of the first carol - *Once in Royal David's City* – with the lights out in a darkened church.

In the recent past the choir has processed, each member holding a lit candle. As the candles flickered, sending shadows dancing on the roof beams, the ladies of the choir sang the first verse unaccompanied, and in my mind's eye I travelled back some sixty-five years.

I was standing but a few feet away, in the aisle outside the curtained vestry at the back of the church. It was cold, very cold for the church was heated by only three electric fires. I was chilled – largely with fear, for this would be my first solo. The note was given and the sound came from my trembling lips, soaring into the roof above.

(Above) St. Peter's in the snow, January 2007.

My voice was wrapped in the warmth of my fellow choristers for the second verse, and with the congregation from then onwards. No candles in those days, but the lights were dimmed as we processed up the church and into the chancel.

No poinsettias, nor Christmas tree, just holly cut freshly from the churchyard – for it was 1944 and the country was weary from war.

But Bob, Ken, Tony and the others were there last night in the shadows, in their black cassocks, white surplices and Eton stiff collars with black bows (fixed with studs that stuck in your neck). The Rev Byng stood nervously by ready – should there be the need – to encourage all the boys to sing that first verse should no note be emitted from my lips. Organist and Choirmaster Mr Butler peered over his glasses with his hands resting on the wooden rail that held the modesty curtain surrounding the organ bench.

As the choir moved up the aisle and into the chancel, and the candles were finally doused with the ending of the carol, the lights came up and the familiar words of the Bidding Prayer echoed down the ages.

Home sixty-five years ago to a house without central heating and a walk through the dark streets of wartime London. Home last evening to warmth through streets where Christmas lights were appearing in gardens and lit trees in windows. Home then to shops with bare shelves and queues. Out tomorrow to shops whose shelves groan beneath the weight of the plenty that we now have.

Life has changed. The world has changed. But are we yet ready *"to hear again the message of the angels, and in heart and mind to go even unto Bethlehem and see this thing which is come to pass"*. I am unsure and as uncertain as ever.

And yet the magic, the excitement, the thrill, the waiting, the warmth, the love that is Christmas is welling up inside me as it has done every year that I can remember.

Carols for the fallen

On the Monday evening before Christmas 2009 a small gathering, led by the Salvation Army Band, sang carols inside the Ilford War Memorial Hall in the Ilford War Memorial Gardens on the A12 near Newbury Park Station. The evening was cold and the air crisp, with the stone floor radiating the chill. A Christmas tree stood in our midst as we trilled through a dozen well-known carols, although the acoustics of the hall meant that the band drowned out our voices except when we sang unaccompanied to give the band members a rest.

It was a strangely moving occasion, quite unlike any other carol singing in which I have been involved. The names of those who had fallen in the First World War had a familiar ring about them. Some of the same names appear on the war memorial in St. Peter's and there are names of families that are still around the area and whose parents and siblings lie buried in the churchyard. I counted eighteen Smiths and eleven Taylors. Remembering those who had given their lives that we might live gave a new meaning to Christmas almost a century on.

History

The history of the Hall is interesting. I am grateful to Foster Summerson who wrote an article for the *London Society Journal* from which some of this material has been culled.

Today the Ilford War Memorial Gardens on the A12 near Newbury Park Station are an oasis of peace, serving as the focus for the London Borough of Redbridge Civic Service on Remembrance Sunday in November each year.

The decision to construct a War Memorial in Ilford was taken at a public meeting on 27th November 1918 – sixteen days after the Armistice - when the Ilford War Memorial Committee was formed to: *"raise subscriptions to a fund to be known as the Ilford War Memorial Fund for the purpose of providing a War Memorial to the memory of Ilford residents killed in the Great War 1914 –1918, and to decide as to the War Memorial to be provided".*

The following year a 'plebiscite' was taken of all residents in the then Ilford Urban District, with 14,000 votes being cast in favour of a Children's Hospital, and to erect a suitable monument. Some £10,000 was raised from donations made by those living in the Borough, local businesses and from those with family or other links to Ilford.

Two acres of land, which form the War Memorial Gardens, were purchased at a cost of £800. The Bronze Sentinel mounted on a Cross was erected at the entrance to the Gardens at a cost of £1,200. This was sculptured by Newbury A. Trent (1885-1963), a member of the Royal British Society of Sculptors and unveiled by HRH Princess Louise on 11th November 1922.

It took another five years before enough money could be raised to build a new wing to the Ilford Emergency Hospital - The Ilford War Memorial Children's Wing – which was built on land adjoining the Memorial Gardens, part of which was purchased by the Fund. The building included the Memorial Hall in which the names of the War Dead would be recorded. The total cost was some £8,000. These were opened by Lady Patricia Ramsey, formerly HRH Princess Patricia, the daughter of The Duke of Connaught and a grand-daughter of Queen Victoria, on 27th June 1927.

Children's Wing

The names of the 1,159 men from the Urban District of Greater Ilford, which included Goodmayes, Seven Kings, Newbury Park, Barkingside and Ilford, who were killed in the Great War are recorded on panels in the Memorial Hall – the original intention being that this would form the main entrance to the Children's Wing. However, other than at the opening ceremony, it appears never to have been used for this purpose. Quite why no one knows, but perhaps a formidable Matron determined that it would be inappropriate!

As a result, apart from occasional use by dignitaries preparing to attend the Remembrance Day ceremony in the inter-war years, the Memorial Hall became an adjunct to the Children's Ward.

It was often used for storage, although on warm days beds were pushed into the Hall and the entrance doors opened to give the children some fresh air.

The Ilford Emergency Hospital became the King George V Hospital and was opened by King George V in 1931. In 1993 that hospital relocated to a site in the grounds of Goodmayes Hospital and is now part of the Barking, Havering and Redbridge NHS Trust.

The buildings of both the hospital and the maternity hospital nearby – which had stood empty for some years - were finally demolished in 2001 to make way for a new housing development.

A campaign was mounted by local groups to preserve the Memorial Hall and a case was made for the building and the monument at the entrance to

(Above) The Ilford War Memorial Gardens – the path from the rear of the Bronze Sentinel in the foreground leads to the Memorial Hall at the back on the right.

the gardens to be added to the statutory list of buildings of special architectural or historic interest (Grade II).

Sadly, it was not possible to get the listing extended to the Children's Wing which was demolished. However, the Memorial Hall, which has a floor area of some 625 square feet was repaired and refurbished by the developers, Bellway Homes Limited, and ownership transferred to the London Borough of Redbridge. The Hall had fallen into serious disrepair. The panels around the walls and the floor were covered with mould which had to be cleaned off. Masonry was cracked, needing expert repair, and the tiled floor required specialist treatment. It was rededicated in August 2005.

In July 2006, the Ilford War Memorial Gardens Action Group was established to improve the gardens and to increase public awareness of their significance as a place of remembrance and for quiet reflection and relaxation. The group comprises representatives of local organisations, remembrance associations, council officers and is chaired by Councillor Ruth Clark. A programme of improvement works was put in hand in the latter part of 2006. Members of the Group have planted spring bulbs – daffodil, crocus and snowdrops – in the beds and in the grassed areas, bringing colour and life to the Memorial Gardens in the springtime. The rose beds have been restocked, new shrubs planted and the flower beds are filled with colour in the summer. Much of this work, which is on-going, has been carried out by members of the Action Group assisted by local residents.

The Gardens were awarded a Certificate of Merit for the most improved public garden by 'London in Bloom' in 2007, and were similarly recognised in 2008. In addition to the horticultural improvements, the railings surrounding the gardens have been repainted and information and interpretative boards erected explaining the history and significance of the Gardens and the War Memorial Hall.

In June 2007, the Action Group organised an Open Day to raise awareness of the War Memorial Gardens and to commemorate the 80th anniversary of the dedication of the Memorial Hall.

A summer concert was held in June 2008 and carol services have been held in the Hall for the past three years – the Hall being decorated with a Christmas tree and holly wreaths.

Funding has also been obtained to provide a small natural play area for young children in a corner of the gardens – and so provide a link that was lost when the children's wing of the hospital was demolished.

Sadly, the Gardens have experienced their share of vandalism and anti-social behaviour, most notably in 2007 when the glass ceiling lantern was badly damaged by stones thrown from the adjoining footpath. The damage has been repaired.

The Gardens are open throughout the day but because of the risk of damage it is not possible to allow unrestricted access to the Memorial Hall.

However, a rota of volunteer stewards has been organised, which has enabled the building to be open to the public on the first Sunday of each month from April to October (2pm to 4.30pm) during 2010 and on the morning of Remembrance Sunday each year.

Adopting the mentally ill

For some fifteen years – from 1991 to 2006 – members of St. Peter's adopted a Ward at Goodmayes Hospital. Initially the Ward was home for elderly patients suffering from mental illness, most of whom had spent all their adult lives in the hospital and, as a result, had become institutionalised – so much so that they would not be able to live outside the confines of the Ward. First it was Hawthorn Ward; later the patents moved to Caroline Ward, which doubled as both a continuing care Ward for the elderly and a rehabilitation Unit for younger patients. The final move was to Martha Ward. All three Wards were housed within the original 1898 main Goodmayes building.

How did it come about that St. Peter's became involved at Goodmayes, which is on the edge of the parish boundary? It can be traced to the following article in the BROADSHEET for December 1990, written by the Rev Michael Trodden, Vicar of St. Peter's at the time:

"As I look back over the last month, I am conscious that I have officiated at some of the most difficult and distressing funerals in the whole of my ten year ministry.

"As you might know, I refer mainly to funerals of very young people, yet I want to talk about one person whom I buried a couple of weeks ago. His name is Alfred McDonald and he was 79 when he died. Why should his circumstances make such an impact?

"I was called out to a Ward in Goodmayes Hospital a few Sundays ago, shortly before Evensong, to say prayers at the side of Alfred who had just died. He had been a patient in the hospital since 1928 when he was admitted - apparently - because he had stolen a dog or a cat.

"During his 62 years (yes, 62 years!) in the hospital he had suffered from hallucinations, which is hardly surprising. Yet he had been one of the most lovely and gentle of men, loved by fellow patients and staff alike.

"The two middle-aged female nurses who were looking after the other nineteen patients on the Ward apologised that they could not join me for a moment, but they had been breaking up a fight - physically - between two large male patients.

"When one nurse did join me she said: *'Do you realise that in coming out for him this evening, this was probably the only time anyone has ever put themselves out for him?'*

"'Pity it was an hour after he died,' I replied.

"Nodding sadly, the nurse said: *'I hope he really has gone to a better place, because he didn't get much down here.'*

"I took Alfred's funeral nine days later and I am sure he would have been touched by the efforts the staff and patients made to give him as good a send off as possible.

"I thought of the words of Christ: *'Blessed are the poor in Spirit for theirs is the Kingdom of Heaven'* (St. Matthew, Chapter 5, verse 3).

"As I returned to my car I had many thoughts - how the psychiatric hospitals seem so often to be the poorest relation in the National Health Service; how people like Alfred desperately need a voice to shout for them; how the staff work with such dedication, yet with so little support; and how some people moan and complain when they just don't know how lucky they are.

"Christmas is coming. We are all about to over-indulge and waste money. This season is all about God's son being born in the humblest of situations for you and me – and for Alfred."

Adopted

Twelve months later – in the BROADSHEET for December 1991 – it is recorded that members of St. Peter's had adopted Hawthorn Ward where

Alfred had died. They had visited the patients throughout the year, decorated the Ward for Christmas, sang carols and collected Christmas gifts – toiletries, socks, hankies, biscuits, sweets. Many made regular cash donations so that each patient received at least one card and a present on their birthday.

Visits to the Ward were made at regular intervals, with the church choir being joined by members of St. Peter's. Singing was the main entertainment, with patients and staff joining in. Whilst we sang a variety of songs, it became clear over the years that the majority of patients – and many of the staff too – enjoyed singing well-known hymns best of all. For accompaniment we relied on a piano that had seen better days. Later Martyn would lead us with the piano accordion, whilst the St. Peter's Morris Team performed on a number of occasions.

Hawthorn Ward will be remembered by many at St. Peter's as the place where a yellow canary sang his little heart out in a small cage slung on a chain from the ceiling amidst the acrid stale cigarette smoke that hung heavily in the air.

A year or two later the patients moved to Caroline Ward. Here we were asked if St. Peter's would help purchase a domestic washing machine to enable some of the younger patents to learn to use this as part of their training in domestic and social skills in preparation for their rehabilitation in the community. Some £400 was collected at St. Peter's and the washing machine was delivered to the Ward in the summer of 1994.

Many of the patients had no-one to visit them and a number of members of St. Peter's struck up friendships, with the patients looking forward eagerly to the next visit. Some would sit throughout the singing, holding the hand of their new found friend for comfort.

The staff, too, became friends. Often they would be busy during our visits, tending to the needs of a patient, but when they were free to do so, some would join in the hymn singing. The Caribbean and African staff and patients especially enjoyed the hymns, singing with great gusto. The staff told us on a number of occasions that the patients went off to sleep more quickly following our hymn singing and often had restful nights – unlike when the Morris Team entertained, for the clashing of their sticks made a few of the patients hyper!

We would take home-made cakes, biscuits, sweets, fruit and other treats for the patents, joining them in a cup of tea or coffee during the evening. One male patient could not get enough home-made cakes – stuffing them into every pocket and disappearing to his bedside before returning to collect some more, all to be consumed later.

Inevitably there were amusing moments. One evening a very good friend at St. Peter's telephoned me at home, asking if he might raise something with me in confidence and, of course, I readily agreed.

"You see," said my friend, "I have a note in my diary for next Tuesday evening. I am to meet Caroline Ward at seven and I have no idea who she can possibly be – and I dare not ask my wife who might think I am seeing another woman!"

We both laughed and were at Caroline Ward at Goodmayes Hospital at seven the following Tuesday evening.

On one occasion Stella left her Burberry raincoat, of which she was very fond, with the coats of the rest of the group of visitors. A few minutes into the singing, Stella saw her Burberry raincoat on the back of a lady patient who was about to beat a hasty retreat into the hospital grounds! That same lady enjoyed visiting jumble sales at local churches, where she invariably bought a hat. She had quite a collection of which she was justly proud – and enjoyed showing off her latest purchase when we next visited Goodmayes.

Three Vicars of St. Peter's – Michael Trodden, Tim Coleman and Clare Nicholson – took an active part in our visits to Goodmayes, all three making themselves available to support staff and patients, whilst Clare accompanied the singing on the recorder. In Michael's time at St. Peter's both he and Jock Mugford, our Reader, led Sunday morning services in the Chapel in the old Goodmayes building. The organ was played by an elderly patient who had – like Alfred McDonald – been incarcerated at Goodmayes for all his adult life. He was a capable organist who loved playing for services, but was quite unable to face the prospect of independent living outside the security that the hospital provided.

For some members of St. Peter's visits to the Wards at Goodmayes were an eye-opener as this was the first time they had been inside a psychiatric hospital. Mental illness has always tended to be swept under the carpet and hidden from public view – and, sadly, this continues to be the case. Getting to know people who were seriously unwell, but who were desperate for friendship, helped some to appreciate more fully the needs of those who suffer mental illness.

We were saddened at the run-down buildings and furnishings, and the lack of therapeutic and meaningful treatment on offer. At the same time we were impressed with the dedication and commitment of the staff, many of whom became personal friends, but concerned that staff often appeared stressed and overworked.

One lady in her 90s from St. Peter's could not get over the fact that the patients were sitting in armchairs or walking about the Ward – and not in bed. This is a hospital, she affirmed, and they should be in bed if they are unwell. Nothing would persuade her otherwise and she only visited once.

At the turn of the Century massive change was sweeping through hospitals for the mentally unwell and with new buildings going up at Goodmayes, the days of the old hospital wards were numbered. Like Alfred, many of the older patients had been hospitalised since their teens. Now those in their

80s and 90s were becoming terminally ill, whilst those with more years to live were assessed and moved to nursing homes where their needs could be met more adequately. By 2006 there were but a handful of patients in Martha Ward when its doors were finally closed.

Whilst there was sadness amongst those who had visited Goodmayes over some fifteen years that this link was coming to an end, there was happiness that the old order had changed and – hopefully - changed for the better. Gone are the days when a teenager would be incarcerated in a mental asylum for stealing a loaf of bread, a dog or a cat, or becoming pregnant, remaining there for the rest of their lives and being unable to fend or care for themselves. Therapies and advances in medication mean that many of those who would in the past have been destined to spend most – if not all – their lives in asylums are now able to live and work in the community. Praise be.

Who are they!

Over the Christmas period the postman delivers bundles of Christmas cards through the letterbox during daylight hours, whilst kind friends who live locally creep up the garden path at dead of night to drop their cards in to us. All great and very much appreciated, for they carry warm wishes for the festive season. But there is just one problem.

From time to time a card will arrive and I am at a loss to work out the sender, but Yvonne steps in and reminds me of their provenance and all is well. Except that on one or two occasions not only am I baffled, but so is Yvonne. It might take us a day or so to work out who 'John' or 'Mavis' can possibly be, but far worse is the 'Fred and Simone' syndrome. I think I might know a Fred or two, but a Fred linked to a Simone is a total, utter and complete mystery. And it is even worse when 'Fred and Simone' also sign for 'Arbuthnot, Miranda and Little Willy'.

Who is the name of all that is good and kind and gentle could possibly have children named Arbuthnot and Miranda, let alone Little Willy? Did we meet them on holiday?

No, because we are not having holidays until we retire (properly) when our child-care duties are at an end. Is it the family that moved in down the road last summer? Hardly likely for if ever I saw anyone less like a Fred, it is him, and she is no Simone, and as for Little Willy!

We are none the wiser days later when yet another poser arrives - this time from Greg and Daisy, who add a footnote to the effect that they long for the old days and trust that our spell in hospital was not unduly taxing.

We are at a loss as to which "old days" they are referring and the nearest we have been to a hospital in the past year was when I caught the 396 bus mistaking it for a 296.

What is really intriguing about all these cards is that they are addressed to "Ron and Yvonne", which proves that *they* know who we are - which is some sort of comfort, I guess.

Unsatisfactory!

We have discovered a photostat copy of my school report dated July 1943, which means that the original must be somewhere.

The document is headed *Borough of Ilford Education Committee, Downshall Middle School, Girls' Department.* Yes, *Girls' Department.*

Now that is worrying, for I am certain sure that I was amongst both boys and girls, but it was wartime so perhaps they had run out of boys' report forms.

My marks for all subjects total one-hundred-and-forty-two-and-a-half from a total of two hundred.

My position in class was twenty out of forty-one on the roll. Individual subject Marks Obtained are as follows, with the Marks Possible in brackets (although I should mention that the actual figures have been inserted in the wrong columns, but perhaps there was a power cut when my Class Teacher was writing up the report and a shortage of candles. It was, as I have said before, war-time).

Arithmetic One 29 (40), Arithmetic Two 21 (40), English General 16 (20), English Composition 10 (20), English Grammar 19 (20), English Spelling 18 (20), Reading 10 (10), History 7 (10), Geography 5 (10), Penmanship 7 (10).

Art and craft is left blank, whilst two subjects are marked with an asterisk as *"Unsatisfactory"* – Arithmetic Two and English Composition.

I consider these marks suspect. Grammar and Spelling have never been my strong points, but Composition and Geography were my best subjects. I demand a recount! (After all, as recorded in my autobiography, *Just an Essex Lad* – now out of print, but possibly about to be reprinted if the demand is there - but worth repeating here, I did win an essay competition in Enid Blyton's *Sunny Stories* at around this time, the prize for which was a hardback copy of the epic tale of *Shadow, the Sheep Dog.*)

But it is the remarks that are interesting. Beside the marks for arithmetic (for we did not study mathematics like today's students) it states: *"Careless in calculations; tables not known well enough; slow in solving problems",* whilst the general comments read: *"Ronald works conscientiously in all subjects but will have to improve to reach standard required by Entrance Examination".*

Signed by Head Mistress E. Stenning, I cannot read the signature of my Class Mistress. I shall retain this document in a safe place until I find the original, when it will be framed for all to see

(Above) This photograph – circa 1928 – shows the hump-backed bridge and Newbury Park Station, together with Railway Cottages, on the Eastern Avenue.

Simple pleasures

I was not around in 1928 when the photograph at the top of this page was taken, but I remember Railway Cottages in the 1930s and have an even clearer recollection of the brick built Newbury Park Station standing proudly on top of the hump-backed bridge over the railway line.

Two wooden shack-like shops may just be seen in the photograph beyond the station – the nearest being the coal merchant's office (where you ordered your coal for home delivery) and the next being Mr Curtis's confectioners and tobacconists (where you could also buy a cuppa and a wad, and sit at small tables covered with American cloth, which was sticky and limp).

The station was similar in construction to the surviving buildings at Barkingside, Fairlop, Grange Hill, Chigwell *et al.* There was a foyer leading over to windows where you stood to buy your ticket and two flights of stairs down to the platforms. The place smelt of smoke and coal, and ash and grime, mist and fog.

Summer Sunday evenings
On summer Sunday evenings in the years immediately following the 1939-45 war, the Eastern Avenue (as we called what is now the A12) was the place to be if you were a young-man-about-town wanting to chat up some talent or a family where the husband and wife were keen to tire out their

young brood to ensure a peaceful night's sleep before work on Monday. With petrol becoming more easily available, cars were appearing on the road again. If you were lucky enough to have a vehicle and petrol coupons to spare, Sunday would find you driving off for the day to the country or to Southend-on-Sea – situated where the Thames Estuary meets the North Sea in a torrent of mud, kiss-me-quick hats, cockles, jellied eels, and fish and chips. And on Sunday evening you would be driving back again – to provide free entertainment to the residents of Newbury Park, Aldborough Hatch and other spots on either side of the Eastern Avenue.

Watching the traffic

It seems remarkable today that sixty or so years ago the pavements along the Eastern Avenue would be crowded with men, women and children on Sunday evenings doing little else other than 'watching the traffic'.

The hump-backed bridge at Newbury Park Station and the whole of the Eastern Avenue had but two lanes of traffic – one going east and the other west. With a build-up of cars returning along the westward lane, a couple of policemen would stand on the bridge, stop the eastbound traffic and signal for the cars returning from Southend to use both lanes. And we just stood and watched and gawped – and watched – and gawped!

Not that we stood still all the time. Often we would sit on a convenient brick wall or wander eastwards from the station to Silverdale Parade, opposite the William Torbitt School. Here there were retail shops of considerable variety – greengrocers, grocers, butchers, ladies' fashions, chemists, bakers, hardware stores, hairdressers, fishmongers. And all had glass windows to encourage what we called 'window shopping'. As dusk came down we walked home to tune in on the wireless (radio to you, Henry) to listen to *Happidrome* with Mr Lovejoy, Ramsbottom and Enoch.

Today we no longer spend Sunday evenings 'watching the traffic' (for the cars speed by too fast) nor do we go 'window shopping' (for the shops at Silverdale Parade have metal shutters to prevent the vandals smashing the plate glass) and *Happidrome* is long, long gone.

Saturday evenings

Our Saturday evenings in the 1940s and early 1950s were spent in one of two ways. We either queued at the Cinema or danced the night away.

We always queued at the Cinema. There were separate queues for the one-and-six-pence and the two-shillings-and-three-pence seats, and I guess there were probably queues for the nine-penny seats, but you did not take your lady friend into that part of the cinema, for those seats were at the very front and you could get a crick in your neck watching Greta Garbo or Clarke Gable in a close clinch or Alan Ladd cavorting across the screen or locked in an embrace.

(Top) The Verger's Cottage, the Church Halls and St. Peter's Aldborough Hatch as I first knew them in the 1940s. The cottage and halls were built in 1867 - four years after St. Peter's was consecrated – as the Aldborough Hatch Church School and sited in the church grounds. The School was closed in 1912 when the building was adapted for use as St. Peter's Church Halls. The halls were enlarged in the 1950s and the cottage was demolished in the 1970s.
(Above) The Church Halls and St. Peter's – photographed on 6th January 2010 in the snow.

St. Peter's Garden Parties were a feature of the social calendar in high summer for many years – held first in the St. Peter's Vicarage garden and meadow, until they were sold off in the 1960s to a developer who built St. Peter's Close whose flats and maisonettes now stand where once there was a lake and lawns and shrubs, and where we camped and sang around the camp fire. After that the Garden Parties moved to Aldborough Hatch Farm and Aldborough Hall Farm (above) with tea, cakes, strawberries and cream on the lawn, sideshows in the meadow and races for the children. After one or two Garden Parties on the green beside the church halls where once the Verger's cottage had stood, Garden Parties gave way in 1980 to the Annual Flower Festivals.

If it was the dancing that took your fancy on Saturday nights, you had the choice of the Palais de Dance (in Ilford Town Centre) or Manor Hall (in upper crust Chigwell).

My sister chose the former whilst my brother opted for the latter. Both took their dancing seriously. Both met their future partners at the dance halls.

My brother worked through a ballroom dancing instruction book by Victor Sylvester, reading the steps aloud as he slid up and down the hall in our home, holding an upturned yard broom to represent his dancing partner.

And me?

I spent my dancing Saturdays at St. Peter's Church Halls, where in the winter we huddled around a single coal fire and in the summer we flung the windows open wide.

The Harmonics played the music.

It was homely and friendly and fun – even if the toilets were outside and Victorian with doors where the wind whistled both above and below.

"Will you cope with the stairs?"

Shortly after I retired I happened to be at a funeral when I met the head teacher of a local primary school. We chatted away – as you do – and the head teacher discovered that I had attended that very same school prior to the outbreak of the Second World War in 1939.

"We are studying the war years," the head teacher told me, *"and it would be good if you were prepared to come to the school to talk to the students"* - something which I readily agreed to do.

Promising that a teacher would telephone me, we went out separate ways.

A few days later a teacher at the school telephoned to ask me if I could attend at a certain date and time.

"How will you get here?" she asked.

"I will walk," I replied.

"Are you sure you can manage that?" the teacher asked and I assured her that I could for I only live a short distance away.

"We could send a car," the teacher said, but I said I would be happy to walk.

"The students will be in the hall on the first floor," the teacher informed me. *"Will you be able to cope with the stairs?"*

I said that I thought I could do so.

But it was the next question which was the stunner!

"We may be studying this period of history at some time in the future," she said – but at this point there was hesitation in the teacher's voice as she paused and seemed to be holding her breath.

Clearly the teacher was uncertain as to how to put the next comment. What she really wanted to say – but did not know how to put it without offending me – was that there was some doubt in her mind as to how long I had to live at my great age and for this reason they would like to make a video recording so that if I died before the next set of students studied this period of history, they would have the video to fall back on.

But the teacher was far too polite and well-brought up to put it so bluntly.

And so she merely asked if I minded if a video was made of what I had to say and, of course, I agreed.

I was met on arrival at the school by the teacher who was in her early twenties. I ran up the front steps and positively bounded up the stairs to the first floor.

I guess that the teacher, in her twenties and fresh from college, must have imagined that anyone who was around during the Second World War would be positively ancient and would need a walking stick at the very least, if not a zimmer frame or one of those electric cars that the elderly drive around on the pavements hereabouts, scaring the living daylights out of those of us who are still able to get around unaided.

Having photographed St. Peter's in all weathers and from every possible angle at ground level over many years, the author decided that he needed a different vantage point for the cover of the 30th Flower Festival brochure – so he ascended the flat roof of the Vestry Room in the Church Halls for this shot in May 2010.

Postscript

Out of the mouths . . .

Chatting to a 15-year-old schoolboy, he enquired – politely: *"What's your job?"*
I pointed out that I am retired, but that I do some part-time examination invigilating.
"I bet that's well paid," said the lad.
"It helps out the pension," I replied.
"And you are retired?" questioned the young man.
"Yes," said I, *"for I am seventy-seven."*
"Wow!" said the boy, somewhat incredulous, *"and you can still walk?"*

Yvonne tried to tempt our grandson Marlon when he was nine into eating new things, suggesting that it would be "yummy" to dip bread and butter 'fingers' into a poached egg.
"That, Nana," said Marlon, *"is not a fact but a matter of opinion."*

And I guess that probably says it all.

List of Photographs

All the photographs, except those on pages 47,48, 57, 59, 69,86, 88 (top) and 89 were taken by the author. We apologise that we are unable to credit the remainder.